MR. & MRS. G.G.

MR. & MRS. G.G.

THE MEDIA PRINCESS AND
THE COURT PHILOSOPHER

FRANK DAVEY

ECW PRESS

Copyright © ECW PRESS, 2003

Published by ECW PRESS
2120 Queen Street East, Suite 200, Toronto, Ontario, Canada M4E 1E2

NATIONAL LIBRARY OF CANADA CATALOGUING IN PUBLICATION DATA

Davey, Frank, 1940–
Mr. And Mrs. G.G.: the media princess and the court philosopher /
Frank Davey.
ISBN 1-55022-565-0
1. Clarkson, Adrienne, 1939– .
2. Saul, John Ralston, 1947– .—Criticism and interpretation.
3. Governors general—Canada—Biography. I. Title.
FC636.C56D39 2003   971.064'092'2   C2002-905420-6
F1034.3.C556D39 2003

Acquisition editor: Robert Lecker
Copy editor: Mary Williams
Design and typesetting: Yolande Martel
Production: Emma McKay
Printing: Transcontinental
Cover design: Guylaine Régimbald – SOLO Design
Front cover photo: Errol McGihan/Ottawa Sun Archives

This book is set in Adobe Garamond and Trajan

The publication of *Mr. & Mrs. G.G.: The Media Princess and the Court Philosopher*
has been generously supported by the Canada Council, by the Government of
Ontario through the Ontario Media Development Corporation's Ontario Book
Initiative, by the Ontario Arts Council, and by the Government of Canada through
the Book Publishing Industry Development Program. Canadä

DISTRIBUTION

CANADA: Jaguar Book Group, 100 Armstrong Avenue,
Georgetown, Ontario L7G 5S4

UNITED STATES: Independent Publishers Group, 814 North Franklin Street,
Chicago, Illinois 60610

EUROPE: Turnaround Publisher Services, Unit 3, Olympia Trading Estate,
Coburg Road, Wood Green, London N2Z 6T2

AUSTRALIA AND NEW ZEALAND: Wakefield Press, 1 The Parade West
(Box 2266), Kent Town, South Australia 5071

PRINTED AND BOUND IN CANADA

ECW PRESS
ecwpress.com

Biography: Respectable pornography, thanks to which the reader can become a peeping tom on the life of a famous person.

—John Ralston Saul, *The Doubter's Companion*

Contents

A Government Job at Last

OR: "You've Come a Long Way, Baby"
 Having Fun
 Cultural Capital in the Capital

Why would I want to write about Adrienne Clarkson and her John? They've never done anything to me. I've never met them—as far as I know. Except as words on newsprint. Never seen Adrienne on television before she became Mrs. G.G., never read her books or John's, never considered reading them. Guess I'm going to have to.

One reason I've never thought much of Ms. Clarkson is that I've never been an avid reader of *Chatelaine*. I've never subscribed to *Maclean's*. I've never stood in a crowd to catch a glimpse of the queen. Never watched much TV, except *The National* and the Weather Channel and a few episodes of *Anne of Green Gables*. Never been to black tie literary dinners in Toronto. I met Northrop Frye once. We were Canada Council jurors together. We agreed to give some money to Matt Cohen, whose fiction Frye admitted he'd not yet read.

I've enjoyed my life not knowing Adrienne Clarkson. She hasn't come to the Nihilist Spasm Band Picnic, which I attend regularly. I take my friendly Great Dane to the Ottawa Kennel Club's annual dog show, but Adrienne has yet to step out of the crowd and ask to pet him. And she's never come to my poetry readings. Neither my dog nor I have missed that. I wrote a bemused book once about Kim Campbell and got myself interviewed on CBC Radio's *As It Happens* and praised by Dalton Camp on CBC Television's *Midday*. I suspect that Dalton knew Adrienne. Maybe he talked to her about my book on Kim.

I feel very strongly about citizenship. I don't let my dogs bark after 10 p.m. I always go out and vote against the worst scoundrel running. When I was a kid in B.C., I hated people with fake British accents, and if I'd been a Quebecker I'd have hated people with fake Parisian accents. I worry that Mr. & Mrs. G.G. may have a little of both. I once lived in Los Angeles, and there I learned to feel even stronger about my citizenship.

Adrienne and John, I read, have been saying a lot of things about citizenship—the kind of things I haven't heard since the days of John Diefenbaker. Quite often, they refer to "we Canadians." The only celebrity my dogs have met is Shania Twain, and they thought she'd make a fabulous governor general. I get worried when I hear people using "we"—my name, your name—that way. It sounds like what I often heard in Los Angeles. I wonder what else Adrienne and John are saying. Or what else the press says they've been saying.

So I'll feed the dogs and start my first run through the public life of Adrienne.

Adrienne Clarkson started her life in Canada as a skinny, penniless, Chinese refugee kid, armed with little else than a hot temper and a yearning for something better. Now it's a ten-room brick house in Rosedale and closets stuffed with French originals, but once it was an Ottawa slum and every school dress sewn at home by mother. (Breslin)

A rags-to-riches mythology seems to have clung to Adrienne Clarkson throughout most of her career—although arguably more because of her riches than her rags. When she was appointed governor general of Canada, that mythology and her "refugee" background were among the first images invoked by the media. "Refugee family arrives in Canada in 1942, against a backdrop of war," wrote the *Toronto Star*'s Judy Steed. A "family odyssey," observed the headline to Juliet O'Neill's article in the *Vancouver Sun*. "Clarkson . . . moved from the margins of Canada's social fabric to its centre," commented a *Maclean's* headline attached to "An Immigrant's Progress," a short autobiographical account by Clarkson. "Once turned away as a refugee," announced the headline to Anne McIlroy's piece in the *Globe and Mail.* Technically, all of these observations were accurate, but collectively they evoked a rather more fraught and cinematic arrival in Canada, and a more Cinderella-like transformation, than those that had actually occurred. Other media voices, such as the *Toronto Sun*'s Stephen Lautens, went even further, suggesting that because Clarkson was from China, her origins must be "humble." Lautens attempted to mock Clarkson with an ill-humoured adaptation of Gilbert and Sullivan, displaying both cultural ignorance and a not-so-covert racism: "An immigrant, a woman and person who is colourful, / Yet for my humble origins my behaviour's imperial."

The Poy family was well off in Hong Kong. Clarkson's mother had to learn to prepare meals for her family after they arrived in Canada, because in China they'd had a cook, among other servants. The Poys were also well versed in British culture and well connected to its institutions. Clarkson's father, William Poy, was not Chinese born. He was born in Australia, in 1907, to a Chinese father, a labourer, who had emigrated there in the nineteenth century, "too late for the gold rush" (as Clarkson explained to Steed). Curiously, neither Clarkson nor other members of her family have made public mention of William Poy's mother, Clarkson's paternal grandmother. They have left unexplained how she came to be in Australia and have not even indicated whether or not she was Chinese, although Jan Wong of the *Globe and Mail* has stated that Clarkson is "one-eighth Irish, through her father" ("Says 'She's Adrienne Clarkson'"); this suggests that one of her father's parents—almost certainly his mother—was half-Irish.

Bill Poy, the eldest of eight children, was educated in English in Australia. He moved to Hong Kong in the late 1920s, where he married Ethel Lam, a woman of the Hakka tribe of China's Taishan province. Ethel's parents were also well travelled, having spent time in Dutch Guyana (now Surinam). As a native-born Australian, Bill would have been considered a British subject— separate Australian citizenship was not legislated until 1949. His Australian birth would have allowed him to return to Australia and given him more complex and possibly more advantageous immigration prospects than those available to Hong Kong-born Chinese.

In addition to being connected to the West by education,

language, and citizenship, the Poy family was connected by religion. Clarkson has written that by the time her family arrived in Canada, they had been Anglican "for several generations," which raises the possibility that one or both of her paternal grandmother's parents may also have been Anglican ("An Immigrant's Progress"). When the Poys made the decision to emigrate, the Anglican and fluently anglophone Bill Poy had been working for the Canadian Trade Commission in Hong Kong for thirteen years (Steed).

Many European men, women, and children captured at this time in China and South Asia were interned by the Japanese in poorly equipped camps in which large numbers died and others suffered the enduring effects of malnutrition. But Poy—because he'd been employed by the Canadian government—was offered a remarkable opportunity to flee to North America. According to Clarkson's sister-in-law, Senator Vivienne Poy, a prisoner exchange was arranged between Japan and the United States. Because the Japanese had fewer U.S. prisoners than the U.S. had Japanese ones, the exchange negotiators asked the Canadian Trade Commission whether it had any local employees who wanted to leave as part of the exchange. The commission provided the Poy family.

When the Poys arrived in Canada, they were informed that they had contravened Canada's 1926 ban on immigration from China, but, as the story goes, Bill argued that the internationally sanctioned prisoner exchange in which they were participating trumped the ban. Government officials decided that the family could stay (O'Neill, "Clarkson's Entry"). Quite possibly, wartime conditions and Poy's Australian birth were also factors in their decision.

When the Poys were granted citizenship, in 1949—two years

after Canadian citizenship came into being—the circumstances were again exceptional. The government had repealed the Chinese Exclusion Act in 1947, but Chinese immigrants who wanted to take the next step and become Canadian citizens still faced discriminatory barriers (as they would until 1967). The Poy family, however, was granted citizenship by an order-in-council (Kareda). A Canadian order-in-council is authorized by statute, issued by a minister or a department, and approved by the governor general. This is a highly unusual way to obtain citizenship, and it's only available to applicants whose cases have, for one reason or another, become too irregular, special, or controversial for normal processes.

Clarkson talked about the circumstances of her family's arrival in Canada in her installation speech and later in her 2001 *Maclean's* article "An Immigrant's Progress," but she remained silent on the subject of the governmental-level connections from which the Poys appear to have benefited. "We did not arrive as part of a regular immigration procedure. There was no such thing for a Chinese family at that time in Canadian history," she told Parliament at her installation. And in *Maclean's* she wrote, "One of the advantages we had as immigrants to Canada was that we spoke English. Coming from Hong Kong, we simply exchanged one blotch of pink on the map for another blotch of pink. What was British, what was colonial, was familiar to us. And as Anglicans for several generations, we had the parish as another community for us besides home and school."

Arriving in Canada, Bill Poy exchanged one Canadian government job for another. The family settled in Ottawa, and Bill went to work for the Department of Trade and Commerce almost immediately. While journalists have described this period as a time of poverty for the Poys, most Canadians would be unlikely to see it that way. Clarkson characterizes the family's first years in Canada as being, for her mother, "a great struggle." She had to learn to cook and to manage the household without servants to assist her. And caring for the children was too much: "She just couldn't cope with me at home, and she begged the school to take me in, even though I was just 4. I started kindergarten in the middle of the year" ("Beginnings").

Clarkson also writes, "although we were never poor, my parents could never have afforded to send me to schools that would have to be paid for" ("Immigrant's Progress")—as if most Canadians could afford to send their children to private schools and the Poys fell short of that norm. The Poys, Clarkson adds, were also taken aback at how much physical space Canadians enjoyed: "we quickly seized upon it after settling in Ottawa, building a cottage nearby in Quebec as soon as we had any savings and spending summers fishing, boating, and living in the wilderness."

Combine this narrative with the one that Urjo Kareda offered of the Poy family's situation in prewar Hong Kong—"Adrienne Louise Poy was born in Hong Kong in 1939 to a world of servants and luxury"—and you get the outline of a life of privilege only briefly interrupted by the undoubtedly terrifying interval of Japanese occupation and the undoubtedly tense and hazardous voyage to Canada across wartime oceans. That life of privilege included the summer cottage in the Gatineaus and, when the time came, a top-quality university education for Adrienne. She didn't have to attend either of the two local institutions of higher learning—Carleton University and the University of Ottawa. Instead, she was sent off to the older and more prestigious University of Toronto—specifically, "Trinity College, with its reputation as the educational playground of the Establishment, a place where you learned your Jane Austen and made your connections" (Kareda). Next, her family was able to provide her with a year of international travel and language study at the Sorbonne. There is no record of young Adrienne holding summer or part-time jobs during this period. "Summers she toured Europe through a trail of museums," writes Catherine Breslin, quoting Clarkson, "from Wales to Leningrad via Czechoslovakia, 'as if it were then or never to do those things.'"

Bill Poy may very well have arrived in Canada with only "his family, a tiny remnant of his fortune, and five meagre suitcases" (Janigan), but he carried with him significant social, linguistic, and intellectual capital. He spoke like a well-educated, native-born English speaker, which in a sense he was. He had a history of service to Canada and connections within the Canadian government (although many fewer than his daughter would come to have). Young Adrienne may have been disoriented to find herself in 1940s Ottawa, a town she's described as, "covered in white snow, filled with white people" (Gatehouse), but her father was well equipped to deal with it. His knowledge of Anglo-American cultural and economic practices would sustain him as a civil servant and enable him to launch a successful import-export business after the war.

Evidently, Bill Poy also possessed an outsider's caution, discipline, and self-awareness, which he passed on to his daughter. Kareda writes, "William Poy's children were raised with a sense of discipline and an awareness of the public presentation of themselves. Speech, diction, grammar, poise, and posture were stressed—all the values, in fact, that we associate with finishing schools for children of the ruling caste. Just as Poy quickly grasped the realities required to re-establish himself in business and rebuild his success, so, too, he gave his children the tools with which they could move forward." Then Kareda quotes Clarkson as saying that her father's confidence in her "is a source of enormous good luck. He'll come and hear my speeches, and maybe correct two little details of grammar—still!"

Perhaps because of his theatre background, Kareda repeatedly stresses the way Bill Poy and his daughter produced or performed themselves, as if life in a new culture was not simply a life to be lived, but a role to be played. Kareda invents a theatrical Clarkson: "Adrienne Clarkson is a consummate performer in the theatre of herself." When he looks at her first years in broadcasting, he remarks, "What she learned was both an extension of her parents' obsession with self-presentation and an exploration of how the system worked and how she could make it work for her."

With the exception of the year she spent as a graduate student/ teaching assistant at the University of Toronto and the eighteen months (from 1987 to 1988) she served as a publishing executive at McClelland and Stewart, almost all of Adrienne Clarkson's employment has been with agencies of the Canadian government. Shortly after becoming governor general, she was asked by the editors of *Maclean's* whether she had "always been a believer in a constitutional monarchy" (maybe those editors somehow assumed that any G.G. would have to believe in such a thing). She replied that she was—"I guess because of the time in which I grew up . . . all my parents' friends were veterans. I lived in Ottawa, which is a government town. It's tied up with all of that" (Lewis and Wallace). Perhaps for similar reasons, Clarkson has always seemed comfortable with government, especially with the roles it has offered and with government-endorsed culture. Her first real job, which she held from 1964 to 1965, was freelance book reviewer for the CBC Television daily afternoon variety show *Take 30*. The opportunity came her way "by accident," through a friend she had made at Trinity (Deakin). In less than a year, the show's producers had offered her the job of co-host.

Two years later, the federal government awarded Clarkson a Centennial Medal, although exactly why and for what—for co-hosting a light-entertainment show?—is unclear. Maybe one of the reasons is that Adrienne had by then married Stephen Clarkson, who was active in the municipal Toronto Liberal Party; according to a 1971 *Chatelaine* profile, Clarkson herself was active in the party. For a full decade, Clarkson served as *Take 30* co-host, gradually gaining national celebrity status. The television audience responded to her apparent warmth, wit, and articulate spontaneity, and her name and face kept cropping up in popular Canadian magazines like *Chatelaine, Canadian Magazine,* and *Saturday Night.* "Do We Need Women's Lib?" *Chatelaine* asked in a November 1970 survey of "Canadian women," and Clarkson was among those invited to field the question. In October 1971, the magazine included her in its list of "105 potential women MPs." *Chatelaine* also featured her as one of the nation's "famous mothers" in July 1972.

Nevertheless, there were strong indications throughout the *Take 30* years and the later CBC period that Clarkson wasn't fully satisfied or engaged with her work. She attempted to establish parallel, more "serious" careers as a print journalist, a fiction writer, and a feminist editor. She published various articles in the *Canadian Forum, Saturday Night, Chatelaine,* and *Maclean's,* many of them about her travels; a book of interviews with married men, *True to You in My Fashion,* in 1971; and two novels, one in 1968, and another in 1970. The tone of the articles is overly formal and solemn. They betray little of the potent mixture of wit, charm, modesty, and confidence that made her such a hit on TV—the quality that, Kareda insisted, allowed her to be a "consummate performer" in portraying herself. The travel pieces mostly record scenes, objects, and people encountered—they are verbal parallels to tourist vacation photos. They show few traces of Clarkson herself as observer or interpreter. On the few occasions she does comment personally, her remarks are clichéd and romantic—as in, "those exquisite birch woods that we see so often in Russian films, white and tremulous in the twilight, eternally and mysteriously young" ("We Took a Turbo-Prop"). Clarkson's Paris is a city whose streets are "crammed with life"; it's a place of "enduring beauty" in which she can feel her "senses quickening" ("Paris").

In a more substantial article about the 1979 federal election, Clarkson praises the "diversity and energy" of Canada, engineers a scene shift by writing "meanwhile, back at the ranch," and concludes by observing that we Canadians "forget to put our mouth where our money is." Throughout all of this, we get the sense of a writer struggling to find a public language in which to establish herself as a serious person engaging in social dialogue. But she's groping among clichés in her search for such a language. In the election article, she inserts an especially self-revealing passage among her sound observations about the fact that women's issues are being suppressed by male condescension: "She who now opens the door and lights her own Virginia Slims, they think, can ask no more. Women are on the national news as reporters, and all's right with the world" ("Opinion Platform").

This, of course, described Clarkson's own situation: she could become a celebrity because she was able to interview celebrities, and she could appear to have influence because she interviewed, reported on, and occasionally socialized with influential people. (How different is that from being a governor general?)

Clarkson's lament about the fact that women were permitted

to come into contact with power but not to possess it gestures towards the more general situation of women in the 1960-to-1975 period. Then, it was very rare for a woman to be a politician, a lawyer, or a medical doctor. It was also relatively unusual for a woman to be employed as a television host or a public affairs commentator or a newscaster. When Clarkson joined the CBC's evening public affairs show *The Fifth Estate* in 1975, she was joining a very small club.

During this time, second-wave feminists were advocating the liberal ideal of equality, declaring that women could perform traditionally male tasks as successfully as men could. For this they were caricatured in the mass media as "bra-burners" and "ball-busters." In their advertising, many manufacturers—such as Phillip Morris, the manufacturer of Virginia Slims cigarettes, which Clarkson had mentioned—congratulated women on having newly achieved a symbolic independence ("You've come a long way, baby!"), but few actually hired women for executive or management positions. University-bound women were encouraged to enroll in arts and education programs, but not in professional programs like law, engineering, medicine, dentistry, architecture, or business. Even in the arts, ambitious young women found themselves, more often than not, serving as typists for crusading male poets rather than becoming seriously engaged artists in their own right. In liberationist politics, they were usually the dedicated supporters of the male leader. Clarkson has herself expressed an awareness of the narrow opportunities open to women in the 1960s (ironically, from the perspective of 1986, she's still referring to those women as "girls"). "I graduated in 1960," she told Kareda, "and I didn't know a single girl in my class at Trinity who went into law school. And now, twenty-five years later, women represent a third or a half."

Clarkson's personal situation throughout the late 1960s and early 1970s reflects this widespread gender disparity. In 1963, she had married Stephen Clarkson of the wealthy accounting clan Clarkson Gordon. Stephen had attended old-money boys' school Upper Canada College, he'd been a Rhodes Scholar and a Woodrow Wilson Fellow, and soon after they married he became a professor of political science at the University of Toronto. It was Stephen who became the Liberal candidate for mayor of Toronto in 1969, not Adrienne; she was merely his most fervent campaigner. It was Stephen who wrote ephemeral books on big important issues (*City Lib: Parties and Reform in Toronto, The Soviet Theory of Development*), not Adrienne; in the same period, she penned her two romantic novels, edited her book of interviews with men on their attitudes towards marriage, and edited the New Woman series for New Press.

Media profiles of Adrienne Clarkson published around this time celebrate the way she managed to combine career and domesticity—they applaud the sexy, provocative television star who was also a devoted housewife. "In addition to being the only current Canadian female TV star," wrote Catherine Breslin, "Adrienne, at 29, is also witty, pretty, sexy, lucky, charming, and depressingly productive. She never makes mistakes. She can even cook and sew." Adrienne and Stephen were, apparently, a "team," and the gap in wealth, power, and legitimacy that yawned between them was of little importance. "In the time she has left over from *Take 30*," Breslin continued, "Adrienne serves as the compleat wife to Stephen Clarkson, a deceptively mild young political science professor at the University of Toronto. As a wife, Adrienne starts her day exercising with Steve (push-ups for him, 10-BX for her), and sometimes ends it sitting in for him at political or editorial meetings. Adrienne and Steve are very much a team, which she credits to the fact that 'basically our marriage is a Christian marriage.'"

In a much more sceptical and perceptive article, which appeared in 1972, Melinda McCracken talked about viewing the Clarksons' "harmoniously" decorated home and recalled how Adrienne had told the press in 1969 that she and her husband "symbolize the new family of the new fast-moving metropolis." McCracken then contemplated Clarkson's many roles—TV star, cosmopolitan traveller, novelist, feminist book editor, wife, mother, and employer of a female housekeeper—summing up with this comment: "She has worked it out so that all the necessities and activities in her life are maintained in equilibrium. She claims she can transcend her situation as a privileged middle-class woman, get beyond it by using her mind. That is, her private world can remain unchanged while she uses it as a base for her other activities."

In light of the poisonous breakup of the Clarkson marriage, which was soon to occur, McCracken's ruminations appeared both poignant and prophetic. As well, although McCracken herself seemed unaware of it, her article revealed a troubled and unhappy dimension to Adrienne's personal life. Clarkson had given birth to a daughter, Kyra, in 1969, and to twin daughters, Blaise and Pascal (named after the seventeenth-century French mathematician and religious philosopher Blaise Pascal), in early 1971. Nine months later, Pascal had died of sudden infant death syndrome (SIDS). At that time, the underlying causes of SIDS were still a mystery, and it was vaguely associated in public discourse with parental neglect and maternal guilt. During an uncharacteristically unguarded moment in the interview, which was conducted in the early summer of 1972, Clarkson told

McCracken that she had just come out of "a deep condition of melancholy . . . It's been going on for about seven or eight months, I guess. And while that's on I can live my life on the surface and cope, but I also know that there's something that's not . . . quite right. But I also know that it'll come back at some point, though it can go on for as long as seven or eight months. I've had it go on for as long as two years." This is not the usual confident Clarkson voice, and it suggests the kind of profound and confused emotions that can strain any marriage. One remedy, of course, is immersion in one's work.

Clarkson's restless casting about for something more substantial to do than afternoon television came to an end in the mid-1970s, about the same time as her marriage was collapsing. In 1974, she was given her own national public affairs show, *Adrienne at Large*. It aired only briefly (from September 26, 1974 to January 2, 1975), but it enabled her to work on political subjects and to travel outside the country. One of the first subjects she undertook was South African apartheid, and for that segment she interviewed novelist Nadine Gordimer and anti-apartheid activist Helen Suzman. In early 1975, she was offered a job that would demand much more of her time and oblige her to travel more frequently: co-host of CBC's new weekly public affairs television show, *The Fifth Estate*.

The demise of her marriage, and her subsequent estrangement from her daughters, must have severely shaken Clarkson's understanding of her own identity. This seems especially likely in light of the way the media had constructed the marriage as part of a wonder-woman image—the image of the media star who is also, as Kareda sardonically exclaimed, a "stylish coiffed-unto-death young celebrity chatelaine." Exactly how the changes in her career were related to Clarkson's evolving personal circumstances has remained obscure, because all parties involved have closely guarded their privacy.

Only one intimate detail about the breakup was ever made public. In 1999, journalist Norman Webster revealed that a "desolated" Stephen Clarkson had said to him as they stood together in a cafeteria line, "Adrienne's left me." In reporting this, Webster added, "Adrienne Clarkson has followed her own star, relentlessly"—implying that such relentlessness may have contributed to her marital difficulties.

Clarkson's move to *The Fifth Estate* and the collapse of her marriage both occurred in 1975. Kareda's explanation of what went wrong is that "the pressure of being a mother and a wife as well as a professional woman in a time-devouring career tore holes in the fabric of her world." Basil Deakin, interviewing Clarkson in 1978, shortly before Stephen Clarkson married Christina McCall Newman, the ex-wife of *Maclean's* editor Peter C. Newman, proposed that "because of the peripatetic nature of Adrienne's work, custody of the children was awarded to the father." Christina McCall formally adopted the girls when they became old enough to consent to it.

By Clarkson's own account, her new job was indeed extremely demanding. She now had no time to play the role of gracious homemaker, which McCracken had witnessed her perform a few years before. Speaking to Deakin, Clarkson confided that *The Fifth Estate* was "an extremely exhausting show. You put in a 14 to 15 hour day." When Deakin asked whether this gruelling schedule allowed her time for "other professional pursuits," Clarkson declared, "None! I'm wiped out by it! The travelling is so intensive. I'm just always on the road and I go from story to story. There'll be people waiting for me at each place, with a day or two's break in Toronto in between." Clarkson's first year at *The Fifth Estate* was especially tumultuous because she and her co-host, veteran journalist Warner Troyer, quarrelled frequently. Troyer resigned at the end of the season.

In 1982, after almost seven years with *The Fifth Estate*—during which she forged useful and enduring relationships with at least some of the celebrities she interviewed—Clarkson left the show to take up the post of Ontario's agent general in Paris. She held that post until 1987. The official story of how she came to be offered this position is that she was headhunted for the Ontario government of Premier William Davis by Caldwell Partners. However, several journalists have suggested that behind the scenes, one of Clarkson's friends, prominent lawyer Julian Porter, who himself had many friends in the province's ruling Conservative Party, worked to ensure that she received the offer. If this is so, then Clarkson's growing connectedness, through both her Rosedale and her CBC encounters, was beginning to bear significant fruit. The appointment, of course, was not only beneficial to Clarkson (who was given a starting salary of $55,000, a lavish and well-located Paris apartment, and an undisclosed but sizable expense account). But it also benefited the provincial Conservatives, because it seemed an imaginative and adventurous move for a government generally perceived as stodgy and pragmatic.

Those writing about Clarkson in this period tended to characterize her as exceedingly hardworking, keeping hours similar to those she kept when she was a television journalist. They also, however, suggested a continuing restlessness. In his June 1986 profile, Urjo Kareda remarked that rumours were circulating that Clarkson would be appointed director of the Canada Council or president of the CBC. He quoted Clarkson herself as saying,

"I don't know what I'm going to do next. I'm going to wait here and finish something. The older I get, the less I worry about what I'm going to do next. Things present themselves and you do them, or you don't. The great troubles I've had in my life have come when I've *insisted*, didn't listen, and went ahead."

But Clarkson did seem to have at least a vague notion of what she wanted to do. A few moments later, she told Kareda that she had been writing a book about her family. She asserted that "the evolution of Canada in the forty years since our family came has been phenomenal," and then she expanded: "I want the world to see that we are in the process of creating something unique in Canada—the first multicultural, bilingual society that *works.*" Clarkson's book on her family, or perhaps on Canadian multiculturalism, has never appeared (she told Susan Carson of the *Gazette* late the next year that although the idea was several years old, it "hadn't ripened yet").

In March 1987, she left Paris, moved back to Canada, and took up the positions of president and publisher of McClelland and Stewart. The company was at the time—and had been for many years previously—the largest and most successful publisher of Canadian trade and literary titles. "I'll be able to run a major cultural institution in the free enterprise field," Clarkson told a Toronto audience in November 1986, shortly after accepting the positions, implicitly acknowledging that "free enterprise" was going to be a new experience for her. "I'm going to hire people and fire people. I'm going to do all sorts of stuff and really have fun" (Moore and Adilman). This certainly was cultural work, but it wasn't necessarily the kind that could be used to advance the cause of Canadian multiculturalism.

It was Clarkson's first nongovernmental job. It was also the first that she didn't excel at. McClelland and Stewart was in financial trouble, and one of Clarkson's stated goals was "to turn it around" (Cameron); she had boasted, "I'm pretty hard-headed about money and about my personal finances" (Moore and Adilman). However, having little publishing experience and no track record in turning a profit (except when it came to her "personal finances"), she found herself in the position of being the least expert of the company's senior editors and management, which included Macmillan of Canada's former publisher and senior editor, Douglas Gibson. An anonymous McClelland and Stewart employee told the *Toronto Star* in May 1988, "She came in with very definite ideas about publishing, about literature in general. People who have been in publishing a long time and know publishing—they resented this woman coming in and telling them how to do their job." According to the *Star*'s Elaine Carey, many of the disgruntled M&S employees, spooked by Clarkson's declaration that she was going to have "fun" hiring and firing, left the company. Clarkson herself was already drifting back to CBC Television, undertaking to co-host a new summer show, *Adrienne Clarkson's Summer Festival.* In September of that year, M&S announced that Clarkson was leaving both jobs. Company owner Avi Bennett would take over from her as president, and the seasoned Gibson would relieve her of her publisher duties. Shortly after this, the CBC announced that her summer show was being repackaged as the regular-season *Adrienne Clarkson Presents.*

The next decade was a relatively quiet one for Clarkson. After a very public period in which she was judged publicity-worthy by the media because the positions she held seemed inconsistent with the image she had earlier established for herself, she attracted little attention. Her television show was deemed a cultural, if not popular, success. The lack of notice suggests that she was perceived as having retreated to the uncontroversial; the secure world of government-subsidized culture had beckoned, and she had abandoned the more challenging world of private enterprise. It's also possible that after Brian Mulroney's Progressive Conservatives were reelected in 1988, the media saw Adrienne Clarkson as a less relevant figure than she'd once been.

That year, she was one of the leaders of a volatile campaign against the Mulroney government and its free-trade proposals, but this was a battle that she and her compatriots would lose. In a 1989 interview with Charlotte Gobeil entitled "Life after Free Trade," Clarkson came across as a public persona partly defined by an issue that was no longer hot. She still sounded unclear about what to do next. She talked briefly to Gobeil about "doing" human rights, but then she swerved away from the idea of helping others and embraced the notion of helping herself. "You do need help from other people. You cannot do everything yourself. You need your friends. You need people who professionally can help you. So where am I going? I don't really know, except to say that I want to streamline what I'm doing so that I can really bring all the threads together."

Gobeil asked her if she'd ever consider going into politics, but Clarkson replied that "the day-to-day life of a politician" held little appeal for her. In 1991, in a brief article she wrote for *Homemaker's Magazine,* she continued to worry about free trade, insisting that "Canada was never about just making money." She protested what she saw as the Mulroney government's preference for the "bottom line" over social programs: "After all these years of putting into place things like our medical plans, our transfer payments to the provinces, our common national cultural institutions like the Canada Council and the CBC, everything is now up for grabs if it doesn't satisfy the bottom line" ("Are We Selling Out?"). An image of former media darling

Adrienne Clarkson as a person who is politically out of favour seems to lurk in the background of these articles.

But, in 1993, the Tories—now led by Kim Campbell—were defeated by Jean Chrétien's Liberals, and the political climate changed yet again. In 1995, after nearly twelve years of rumours that Clarkson was on the verge of being awarded a high-profile job in cultural administration, Chrétien named her chair of the Canadian Museum of Civilization, in Hull, Quebec, and the Canadian War Museum, in Ottawa. In this position, which she would shoulder on top of her producer and host duties for *Adrienne Clarkson Presents,* she also received very little public attention—that is, until she announced plans for the War Museum's long-awaited new building. The plans included a large Holocaust gallery that would take up as much as twenty-three percent of the museum's display area. Why? Possibly because certain wealthy donors were willing to help finance the construction of a new building with such a gallery. Or possibly because Clarkson and the museum board viewed—not unreasonably—the Holocaust as a major part of Canada's military history.

The detailed story behind the Holocaust gallery plan has never been made public, but Clarkson's announcement provoked the ire of veterans' groups and of those who—like journalist Les Peate—claimed to represent veterans. Peate, writing for *Esprit de Corps,* a magazine for Canadian soldiers and veterans, vigorously protested the whole endeavour, claiming that angry veterans had exposed "much dirty laundry . . . including the fact that two million bucks in donations to the Museum building fund from Jewish sources hinged on a Holocaust gallery." An accompanying article by Norman Shannon accused Clarkson of "contempt of Senate" and of manipulating Senate process in order to prevent discussion of some veterans' wishes to see the War Museum become independent of the Museum of Civilization. *Esprit de Corps's* view of Clarkson as a Parliament Hill insider was not one that was widely circulated or known to her CBC audiences, but under the circumstances it seems plausible. Clarkson herself made no public statement about the issue.

A year later, Prime Minister Chrétien appoints Clarkson governor general of Canada. The job is a good one in terms of some of its fringe benefits—house, transportation, staff, enormous garden. Clarkson had come a long way from having to rely on a single housekeeper, as she'd done when she was married to Stephen Clarkson. Rideau Hall, Barbara Yaffe writes, has "a staff of about 130 . . . and costs nearly $3 million annually to run." The governor general also has a spacious suite in "the Citadel in Quebec City, which costs about $440,000." The travel and hours, however, are as onerous as those of the co-host of *The Fifth Estate*. In her first year alone, Clarkson spoke in more than forty Canadian cities, from Iqaluit, Victoria, Banff, Saskatoon, Brandon, Toronto, Jonquière, and Sydney to St. John's. At each stop, she had to deliver one or more five-page speeches, and she had to pitch many of them to an audience that had never watched *Adrienne Clarkson Presents*.

Maybe we should ask the classic detective question: Who stands to profit from all of this? Who profits from the fact that Clarkson now holds the ultimate Canadian government job? Maybe it's Clarkson herself: as G.G., she can fulfil her desire to "do" human rights at very little personal expense. She gets to hand out "Bravery Awards" or "Caring Canadian Awards" and talk about "how far" Canada has come, measured by how far a "skinny refugee kid" has travelled—from a working-class Ottawa neighbourhood to Rideau Hall. Or maybe it's Canadians in general who profit: with Clarkson as G.G., our tolerance of multiculturalism may increase another micron; obliged to recognize Clarkson's Chineseness, we may be obliged to think about what it means that within decades a Chinese woman went from being one of the least desirable of Canadians to one of the two or three most prestigious. The major winner, however, seems to have been Jean Chrétien. For almost six months, the public's interest in Clarkson and the novelty of her appointment deflected attention from the stagnation of his government and the unhappiness of his powerful minister of finance, Paul Martin. Because Clarkson had never been elected to anything and had been associated with such seemingly nonpolitical concepts as entertainment, beauty, art, and literature, Chrétien profited from the illusion that he'd made a nonpartisan appointment. Because his appointee was Chinese and female, he also profited from the illusion that he'd in some way redressed past injustices—although the claims of the Chinese head-tax payers and their heirs remain unsettled. The prime minister profited as well from the fact that those who criticized the appointment would leave themselves open to charges of racism. It's the same principle that Clarkson herself relied upon when she parried questions from journalist Trevor Lautens about her arguably expensive hotel accommodations in Victoria, B.C. Lautens reported that the new governor general had implied that he wouldn't have asked her such questions "if it weren't for her gender (female) and race (Chinese)." (Lautens, however, weakened his own antiracist credentials by saying that Clarkson had chosen "to blather about Louis Riel" and by concluding with an angry reference to "her petulant self.")

Chrétien's advantages weakened as Clarkson's time in office lengthened. In the first year, media attention was intensive, and Clarkson's name and photograph appeared in the front sections of Canadian newspapers several times weekly. Many of the articles focused on Clarkson or her husband, or they weighed the merits of her appointment rather than merely detailing the viceregal duty she was performing. By the second year, however, weeks could pass without such a piece appearing. Most of the articles that were published covered awards she had presented; there were also a few news items—such as the death of the Princess Margaret—in which she had played a small part. Many of these were buried deep in the paper.

There is nothing especially significant about this change. Some of it is attributable to Clarkson's remarkable effort in her first year to make herself and her new office known to Canadians in all parts of the country and some to the fact that the novelty of her appointment was time-limited. By mid-2002, she was, to most people, simply the governor general. When Pope John Paul visited Toronto for World Youth Day in late July, he squeezed brief meetings with Clarkson, Chrétien, and Ontario premier Ernie Eves into his crowded Saturday schedule. An extremely short CBC Television clip shows Clarkson sitting elegantly to the pope's right, facing the cameras and smiling. The pope looks impatient, and he starts to tap his hand on the right arm of his chair to get Clarkson's attention. He has other people to meet, including Chrétien and Eves, and 200,000 youth delegates to address later in the day. Somewhat startled but still smiling, Clarkson swivels abruptly, and with intensely focused vivacity she speaks to the pontiff. It's as if she's trying to make up for having been caught treating the occasion as a photo op. For the following two days, the major papers run large colour photos of the pope, as they had for most of the preceding week—but there are none of the pope and Adrienne Clarkson.

TAKE TWO

Media Royalty

OR: Queen for Life
     Trusted, Connected, Canadian

It seems that I've assembled a collage of press clippings. A collage of Adrienne Clarkson's life. My editor wants to know what goes on in the semiroyal Rideau Hall kitchen. When your life is producing images for the media, is there life—perhaps a grilled organic Canadian Cheddar sandwich—behind the media? The question isn't just who or what is Adrienne Clarkson, but who or what is the new, viceregal Adrienne Clarkson. Why do we have an ultimate Canadian job? Why do we have a queen (whom I've never stood waiting for by the roadside)? Do I have to like a royal if I happen to agree with the sentiments of her hypocrisies?

> To flaunt the fact that kings are capable of prosaic actions is to recognize that this status is no more natural to them than angelism to common mortals; it is to acknowledge that the king is still king by divine right. (Barthes 32)

The idea of royalty begins in a complex interaction—among individual assertions of power and group desires for continuity, significance, and stability. Societies need leaders, and leaders, whether they be Jean Chrétien or Zimbabwe's Robert Mugabe, enjoy the processes and perks of staying in power. At its extreme, the idea of royalty produces myths of superior blood and divine ordination. These myths are, of course, pretensions, but because royals and their cronies find them handy for explaining and preserving their privileges, they take them very seriously.

Historically, the first in a line of monarchs has usually been a usurper, a conqueror, or a tyrant—like England's William the Conqueror, or William and Mary of the Glorious Revolution of 1688. His or her successors enjoy rank, privilege, and land tenure until another successful usurper, conqueror, or tyrant temporarily disrupts the tradition of royal succession. In recent times, we've witnessed that pattern in the families of Lebanese warlords, in Kim Jung Il's succession to his father Kim Il Sung in North Korea, and in Bashar Assad's succession as president to his father Hafez Assad in Syria. It doesn't matter that the inheritor isn't always as wily or as ruthless as his predecessor, because his succession both symbolically and practically protects the interests of the same set of individuals and institutions. If he can compound this by projecting an image of himself as a ruler who enhances the well-being of his people—even if it's only their emotional well-being—then he will further strengthen his hold on power. Something like this happened within the U.S. Republican Party when George W. Bush succeeded his father, George Bush, as the party's presidential nominee.

In Canada, royalty was installed with the first European "discoveries" and settlements. The French and British monarchs of the sixteenth and seventeenth centuries claimed power over the land and the indigenous populations of North America. The early inscriptions of that power remain to this day: Montreal—literally, "Mount Royal"; Louisbourg, the fortress city built by Louis XV in Nova Scotia; Jamestown, Virginia—named after James II of Britain and Elizabeth I, England's "virgin" queen; Charleston, South Carolina—named after Charles II of Britain (doubly, since Carolina derives from the Latin form of Charles). Canadians also have the Hudson's Bay Company, incorporated in 1670, thanks to a grant from Charles II that included all North American territory draining into Hudson Bay (land that Charles presumed to own and control). The first North American governors, and later lieutenant-governors and governors general, served as administrators of the legal systems established by those initial raw assertions of power. These assertions were effectively conquests, although the indigenous peoples may not have understood the symbolism of the planting of European flags on North American territory until the conquest had become what our own age calls "facts on the ground."

Today, the rights of Canadians to own land rest on the legal fiction of "crown land," on the sale or granting of crown land, and on a continuity of title that can be traced back without break from owner to owner to the crown, and in most cases to the documented "surrenders" of lands to the crown by indigenous peoples. Canadian civil rights rest on the 1982 Constitution and

Charter of Rights, on English common law, and on the Magna Carta conceded to and signed by King John in 1215.

The governor general in twenty-first-century countries such as Canada, Australia, and New Zealand is a symbol of this continuity of institutional power. It is a power founded at various mythological moments of assertion: Cartier's planting of a cross and the French coat of arms on the shores of the Baie de Gaspé in 1534, Charles II's granting of a charter to the Hudson's Bay Company, Pierre Trudeau and Queen Elizabeth II's signing of the 1982 patriated Constitution and Charter of Rights. Images derived from such moments have become Canadian icons: François Riss's paintings of Cartier's landing (reproduced on a Canadian postage stamp in the late 1980s), Benjamin West's painting of the death of General James Wolfe, the red-coated *Royal* Canadian Mounted police officer, the postage-stamp image of the Fathers of Confederation at the 1866 Charlottetown Conference, the photograph of Trudeau watching Elizabeth sign her name, the photographs of Adrienne Clarkson arriving in the royal landau to open Parliament. I could make another collage.

So the power of enduring royalty rests on raw power. But it also rests on the fantasy of love and on the public relations fictions that the "beloved leader" or "big brother" manages to circulate. The good King Wenceslas myth of royal benevolence has always been carefully fostered by the wise ruler-for-life: the "good King Harry" image created by Henry VIII, or the poster image of himself as teacher, builder, caregiver, counsellor, grandfather that Saddam Hussein has foisted on contemporary Iraq. When rulers are careless about the myth of royal goodness, their power may collapse. Such carelessness toppled the Stuart kings of England in the seventeenth century, the Bourbon kings of France in the eighteenth century, and the Shah of Iran in the last century.

For rulers like these, who exercised executive power, "goodness" could be created or damaged in a complex, interlocking array of arenas such as the economy, personal expenditure, criminal justice, patronage, health, education, religion, and war—the same arenas in which today's parliamentary governments create or destroy their own images of goodness.

For a monarch in a parliamentary democracy, goodness is mostly a matter of the management of public image. Even when the public is aware of a possible dissonance between the private self and the constructed image, the public will, for the most part, be satisfied by displays of dutiful hypocrisy. Thus, the wise princess wears a fashionable hat to the races at Ascot one day and presides over the opening of a new hospital wing the next. She has her photo taken with AIDS patients. The wise prince expresses concern about ecological change. In her annual Christmas message, the fabulously wealthy Queen Elizabeth deplores the deaths of innocents in civil unrest and, by implication, the uneven distribution of wealth from which such unrest usually stems. The power that such goodness protects is the power of wealth, privilege, and social status—a power incarnate in the royal lands and palaces, art collections, horses, ceremonial titles, and servants (such as the sixty-five that maintained the queen mother in her last years). This wealth has been assembled over the centuries by means of what we currently call cronyism, nepotism, conflict of interest, insider information, unjust enrichment, influence peddling, regressive taxation.

The perceived goodness of some Canadian governors general, however, has benefited the Canadian state—and, indirectly, the government in power—much more than it has the British royal family, for which the governor general stands in. A "caring" governor general symbolizes for most Canadians a caring national state—one that rushes to the aid of its soldiers when they are injured, that remembers its war dead, that honours its heroes, and that values its history and its achievements. When Adrienne Clarkson hastened to Germany in April of 2002 to meet Canadian soldiers injured in Afghanistan, Canadians felt good (judging by an informal survey of letters to the editor), not about the British royal family, but about themselves and their country. The effect was parallel to the one created by the late queen mother during the Battle of Britain, but this one enhanced Canadian rather than British institutions.

In recent times, the fantasy of royal love hasn't rested entirely on the royal individual's generalized love for "the people." Sometimes, it has rested on the royal's capacity to offer love in a more specific and immediate way. Queen Victoria's ostensible love of her children was expanded into the Great White Mother image, which Canadian treaty negotiators extended as a psychological promise to native peoples. Here, too, the myth of love benefited not Victoria or her family, but the Canadian state. Victoria's apparent love of her husband, Prince Albert, and the years she spent publicly mourning him, allowed her public to indulge in fantasy identification with her as an extension of their own loving and mourning selves. The late queen mother offered her public both fantasies. She was the good queen who cared for her subjects during World War II; remaining in London with her family, she made public "motherly" displays of concern for the inhabitants of bomb-devastated neighbourhoods. Later, her mourning of her husband, her affection for her "favourite grandson," Charles, and her cheerfulness in the face of illness and old age gave rise to fantasies of identification—fantasies of "Queen Mum," the mother we would like to have, or be.

Prince Charles's popularity plummeted when he allowed people to perceive him as uncaring towards his ex-wife, Diana, and insensitive to the feelings of their sons when she died. It plummeted still further at her funeral, because he allowed Diana's brother to appear more "loving" than any of the core royals. But it rose in 2002, when he expressed on television, in a seemingly intimate manner, his affection for his late grandmother.

For a king or ruler with actual power, it's an extremely complex task to maintain a firm hold on the love of the people. It depends on a myriad of interlocking approaches in economics, education, health, foreign policy, religion, cultural policy, military policy, and criminal justice. This is one of the reasons that Saddam Hussein has projected multiple images of himself. It also partially explains the difficulties of the Stuart kings amid the conflicting cultural currents of the English seventeenth century. For the constitutional monarch, the task is simpler—it involves manipulating images rather than managing real issues. However, the constitutional monarch still has to balance personal substance with symbolism. For Charles, the decision to marry Camilla Parker-Bowles may be primarily a question of image, but it's also an important personal decision; for Edward VIII, the question of whether to marry Wallace Simpson had the same dimensions. That is, the maintenance of a favourable or "beloved" public image is not always consistent with the indulgence of a royal's personal desires. Traditional commentators see such inconsistency as a conflict between duty and self. But it's more reasonable to see it as a choice from among self-fulfilling options—a choice of whether to be more or less loved by various people. As Abraham Lincoln, another public figure who faced image choices, knew, you cannot please all of the people all of the time.

Being loved has become a prerequisite for success in Western society. Contemporary royalty's problems with being loved and admired are shared by biscuit manufacturers, by toilet paper manufacturers and their "charmin" images of defecating bears, by media producers, and, especially, by media figures themselves. The British royal family, like any other modern communications enterprise, has its public relations counsellors. Much of what royalty presently does can be described as producing entertainment spectacle. The daily changing of the guard at Buckingham Palace attracts spectators in the same way that a free street performance by Ricky Martin or the Barenaked Ladies attracts spectators on Toronto's Yonge Street. And in each case, the performance can build goodwill among those who enjoy it. Prince Charles and his sons ski in the Alps for the benefit of the paparazzi; in Hollywood, minor stars leave their footprints in wet cement in order to get their pictures into hundreds of newspapers.

The royal spectacles—the queen arriving in her grand coach to open Parliament, royal funerals, coronations—function much like those of the entertainment industry. Consider Céline Dion's Las Vegas remake of her wedding, or the annual self-adulation festival that is the Academy Awards. All are lavish visual rewards for the faithful, and they confirm the significance of both the watched and the watching. As David Cannadine has observed, royal spectacles are now rigorously planned, rehearsed, and presented to the public as if they were faithful reproductions of ancient ceremonies, which they are not, for even a hundred years ago such events were chaotic, ill-planned, and often improvised on the spot.

There are, however, important differences between royal celebrity and common celebrity. Royal celebrity can't be sought or avoided. A royal is born into celebrity; it's a condition of his or her existence. While Garbo could succeed in being "alone," Princess Margaret never could. Royal celebrity can also be a central aspect of national identity: contemporary Britons of all classes find it impossible to imagine a Britain without a royal family (Billig 29). Simply by being born into celebrity, the royals participate in, and help construct, for the British a fictitious national identity that they can imagine back to Anglo-Saxon times and forward into an otherwise uncertain future. Conversely, common celebrity is usually sought, and the celebrated person is often someone who has desired fame, who aspires to wealth or other distinction, who thinks himself or herself entitled to a higher status. Would-be celebrities must draw attention to themselves—by wearing quirky or stunning clothes on Academy Awards night, by taking a provocative stand on social issues, by trashing more established rivals in the national media. Would-be celebrities can thus be accused of narcissism, ambition, and hubris—accusations that are rarely levelled at royals.

The acceptable range for spectacular behaviour, however, is much narrower for British royalty than it is for commoners. There is little reward for being a royal version of Kurt Cobain, Janis Joplin, or Screaming Lord Sutch—as the relatively modest efforts of the Duke of Windsor, Princess Margaret, and Princess Diana have demonstrated. Royal celebrity must meet the expectations of a diverse public. It must reflect tradition and flexibility, continuity and responsiveness to changing times. There is only small symbolic profit for royalty in appealing to niche audiences that might appreciate surly rebellion or melodramatic self-destruction. Of all the royal "rebels," only Diana attracted widespread sympathy and approbation. She didn't do this by defying tradition. She did it by constructing herself as the injured wife, the devoted mother, the conscientious citizen who visited AIDS hospices and old battlefields to campaign against land mines—all relatively soft mainstream images.

Although structurally Canada is a constitutional monarchy similar to Britain and headed by the same queen and royal family, the place of the royal family in Canadian culture is significantly different. There is very little linkage between the royal family and Canadian nationalism. In fact, Canadian nationalism has frequently been expressed by the steps the government has taken to dissociate the country from the monarchy. We can see that pattern of increasing dissociation in various governor-general appointments over the years: a Canadian-born governor general in 1952; a Canadian-born, francophone governor general in 1959; a Canadian-born, anglophone governor general of non-British ancestry in 1979; and, most recently, a Hong Kong-born anglophone of nonwhite ancestry. The queen's portrait may appear on Canadian coins, but Canadians rarely use the word "our" when speaking about the monarchy—as in, "our queen," "our royal family." On much of Canadian paper currency, portraits of nationally affirmative prime ministers such as Macdonald and Laurier have long displaced that of the queen.

Most often, stand-ins for royalty in Canadian nationalism are people linked to specifically Canadian institutions. These institutions provide a temporal continuity that individual Canadian celebrities cannot possibly possess. A few prime ministers, most recently Pierre Trudeau, have managed to shake off the conflict and pragmatism of politics and become iconic representatives of the nation. To date, Trudeau's state funeral was arguably the Canadian cultural event that has most resembled, in pageantry and national response, the great theatrical weddings and funerals of British royalty. The occasion was even marked by the theme of hereditary continuity: journalists responded to the funeral oration of Trudeau's son Justin by suggesting that he might soon enter politics.

But the most effective Canadian national symbols, which perform the same role as Britain's royal family, are institutions such as the Royal Canadian Mounted Police, the Canadian Pacific Railroad, the older Canadian universities, the Canadian Broadcasting Corporation, the Trans-Canada Highway, and, more recently, Medicare, Canadian literature, bilingualism, and multiculturalism. Individual celebrity has advanced itself through association with these institutions: Gordon Lightfoot made such a linkage by composing "The Canadian Railroad Trilogy"; Margaret Atwood by writing *Survival: A Guide to Canadian Literature*; Don Messer, Lorne Greene, Peter Mansbridge, and Adrienne Clarkson by acting as the voices of the CBC; Pierre Trudeau and Céline Dion by, in very different ways, symbolizing the mid-twentieth-century Canadian bilingual ideal.

The institution of Canadian literature has been modelled on British literature, which, in the last three hundred years, has constructed Shakespeare as a timeless icon of Britishness. Since about 1960, CanLit has provided Canadians with the same national symbolism of continuance and modest change that the royal family has provided so superbly to the British. Canada's "timeless" literary icons are almost entirely female: Lucy Maud Montgomery and her *Anne of Green Gables;* Margaret Laurence and what she called her Canadian "tribe" of fellow writers; "CanLit queen" (as she's often identified by the media) Margaret Atwood, whose *Survival* invented a myth of Canadian national continuance. The words *tribe* and *queen* indicate the writer's desired relationship to the hereditary-lineage role played in British nationalism by the queen and her family.

Another institution that has both persistently constructed itself as national and been so constructed by others is the Canadian Broadcasting Corporation, the CBC. Its current motto, sonorously intoned before many of its broadcasts, is "Trusted, Connected, Canadian." The implication is that other Canadian-owned television networks are neither "trusted" nor especially "Canadian." It is not without reason that for decades it has called its flagship news program *The National*. A succession of its news anchors—Lorne Greene, Lloyd Robertson, Knowlton Nash, and currently Peter Mansbridge—have become figureheads for the nation, offering visual continuity that outlasts governments, prime ministers, economic cycles, and foreign military involvements. In the same way that the British see their royalty as outlasting prime ministers and transcending party politics, Canadians can see their national news anchor—never flashily dressed, subliminally Mr. Average Canadian Man—as objective, commonsensical, authentic, in contrast to the evasive and posturing politicians whom he often questions.

This continuity deficit in politicians, which causes even prime ministers to be associated with temporary pragmatic measures rather than with enduring national achievements, has limited the effectiveness of the Canadian governor general's office as a national symbol. Most of Canada's Canadian governors general—with the possible exception of Vincent Massey—have been mere stand-ins for the monarch. They are people who had little national celebrity status before the appointment, enjoyed the status of the position while they held it, and faded into the shadows afterward. Most have been minor politicians—federal cabinet ministers, a provincial premier. Most, also, have been inoffensive people with a bland history of public service. The entertainment and media counterparts of such figures are middle-of-the-road in terms of class, age, sexuality, politics—Anne Murray, say, rather than Alanis Morrisette or k.d. lang; Bryan Adams rather than Ashley MacIsaac.

In a legal and technical sense, of course, there doesn't have to be a direct association between the office and the person who fills it. In the Christian faith, the priest is a stand-in for Christ, and during Communion he reenacts the actions of Christ. Each priest performs the rites of the church with equal theological effectiveness, no matter how confused or blameworthy he is in his personal life. This is because it is the office, not the priest, that performs these rites. Similarly, the governor general is a stand-in for the monarch, who herself stands in for the Crown as a symbol of the continuity of the state. No matter what the individual qualities of the monarch or the governor general—be that person a cheat, a liar, an adulterer, a narcissist, or a drunkard—the acts they perform and the awards they give are effective and legal.

In a practical sense, however, the institutions of a democracy function best when they have the support of the public. Victorian economist Walter Bagehot first noted this in 1867, when he recommended to British monarchs, who no longer held any administrative role, that they focus on offering the public "dignified" spectacles and on acting as "a visible symbol to those still so imperfectly educated as to need a symbol" (82, 90). This advice to become "a visible symbol"—in effect, a benign celebrity—is at the root of the contemporary British royal family's concern with image, pageantry, and ritual, and its intermittent focus on public caring.

Apart from the constitutional presence, an ocean away, of the British royal family, Canada has no institutional celebrities. Governors general symbolically stand in for the monarch for a five-year term and are—unlike even a monarch who abdicates—separated from that royal symbolism at the end of the term. However, Canada does have entertainment and cultural industries,

industries in which the British royal family have, since Bagehot, been increasingly participating. The monarch's command performances—such as the one recently held by Elizabeth at Buckingham Palace in celebration of her Golden Jubilee—strongly resemble a production such as *Adrienne Clarkson Presents,* which itself has resembled the Canada Day variety shows on Parliament Hill, also televised by the CBC.

The slow convergence of the royal family "firm" and the British entertainment industry, demonstrated by such events as Elton John's performance at Princess Diana's funeral, has conferred quasi-regal status on all Western entertainment industries. Prince William and Madonna appear in separate panels on the cover of the same magazine. The same paparazzi that pursued Princess Di now pursue Britney Spears. The "personalities" produced by Canada's few continuing national institutions, especially those associated with culture and entertainment, become Canadians' own quasi-royal celebrities—"queen" Margaret, "regal" Adrienne, "queen" of soft jazz Diana Krall, Céline Dion and her mock-royal Egyptian wedding. Nationalist feelings similar to those experienced by the British towards the royal family—"The country just wouldn't be the same without them!"— attach themselves to such figures. Such feelings, in turn, become associated with personal identification, in the sense that our national identification as Canadians is partly defined through the lives of particular celebrities.

Canadians do not harbour these feelings for the British royal family. During the queen's Golden Jubilee celebrations, several Canadian news organizations attempted to survey Canadians about their attitudes towards the monarchy. In early February 2002, the *Toronto Star* conducted an on-line survey that elicited only nineteen responses in three days. The nine nationalist respondents all favoured discarding the monarchy on the grounds that Canada is a "grown-up," "multicultural country," and that having a monarchy is "degrading." Three other respondents disapproved of the monarchy on the grounds of class, using words that have also been used by some Canadians against Clarkson: "arrogant," "freeload," "money," and "phoney lifestyle." Some respondents were indifferent: the monarchy was okay in the past but is no longer "meaningful"; it's as nice as "morning coffee" but not really necessary; Canadians have come a "sad distance" from it, and they now need something "to replace our old loyalty." Two of the four positive responses emphasized the monarchy's constitutional role: it can prevent Canadians from enduring national "shame," like the shame the U.S. suffered after Watergate; it can keep an "elected individual" from going "the way of a dictator." Another invoked heritage; the fourth expressed "love" for the queen. By contrast, Billig, in 1992, found that the vast majority of Britons desired to retain the monarchy for nationalist reasons; these included preserving national identity and keeping Britain distinct from the U.S. While most Canadian antimonarchists in the *Star* survey were nationalists, most British antimonarchists invoked class.

In a more formal poll, conducted for the *Toronto Star*/CTV/ EKOS Research and published in May of 2002, Canadians appeared split fifty-fifty on whether to keep the monarchy. Fifty-five percent agreed with the statement that the monarchy distinguishes Canada from the U.S., but the survey did not ask respondents how important this function was to them. Fifty-two percent agreed that the monarchy is "an outdated and regressive institution that has no real relevance to most Canadians today," and only thirty-three percent disagreed. Asked to choose two adjectives that best describe the monarchy, fifty-nine percent selected "tired," fifty-two percent chose "interesting," forty-six percent selected "relevant," forty-four percent chose "irrelevant," thirty-five percent chose "boring," and only twenty-two percent selected "vibrant." More significant, only five percent of the 1,217 respondents were aware that Queen Elizabeth is Canada's head of state (Graham Fraser).

Direct and indirect expressions of nationalism were frequent in the media responses to Clarkson's appointment. Almost every news story took note of Jean Chrétien's insistence that Clarkson constituted a "reflection of the diversity and inclusiveness of our society"—that is, she symbolized a multicultural Canada—even when the journalist writing the story disapproved of this characterization of the country. Many presented the prime minister's words as their own. Juliet O'Neill of the *Calgary Herald* wrote approvingly of "the symbolism of her appointment as the first immigrant governor general" ("Broadcaster"). Robert Lewis, editor of *Maclean's,* editorialized that Clarkson and John Ralston Saul "may be able to project important and quintessential Canadian values. As an immigrant and refugee herself, Clarkson sends a positive message about the merits of industry and tolerance." Michael Valpy of the *Globe* wrote that the "job would appeal to" Clarkson because of "all its symbolism and potential for weaving a tapestry of the country." But Valpy did add, in deference to his own conservative and immigration-nervous views, that Canada is "a country becoming harder to love because it's becoming harder to find." Judy Steed of the *Toronto Star* titled her story about the appointment "A Classic Canadian Dream," as if the national symbolism of the appointment were self-evident. In the *Calgary Herald,* a paper that had expressed mixed feelings about Clarkson's elevation, Joan Bryden quoted a remark that Massey College's John Fraser made about Clarkson: "She has an incredibly strong sense of identification with Canada." Richard Foot, in a *National Post* article generally unfavourable towards Clarkson, quoted political science professor Peter Russell, who suggested that the new governor general might become a "symbol" of Canada, "an individual who sums up what makes us interesting as a people" ("Challenge"). An editorial in the Montreal *Gazette* declared that Clarkson could transform the governor general's office into "one that can help in the process of nation building." A *Fredericton Daily Gleaner* editorial pronounced her appointment "a splendid reflection of Canada's modern multicultural makeup."

Of those who were critical of the appointment, some also mentioned nationalism, but they did so in the context of their disapproval for Clarkson's long-known nationalist ideas. Clarkson, "a staunch advocate of Canadian economic and cultural nationalism . . . yesterday designated to serve as the Queen's representative," is the way Robert Fife began his story in the *National Post* ("Activists").

The "royalty" criterion was also frequently mentioned in these responses, but much less often than Canada's nationhood was. While a few of the mentions were positive, the majority were not; the negative ones tended to be longer and more emphatic than the positive. In these references, Clarkson was cast either as appropriate for the job because she was among the most "regal" of Canadians, or as inappropriate for it because of her antidemocratic, quasi-regal pretensions. The *National Post*'s Rosemary Sexton was pleased because Clarkson would bring "panache" to the office of governor general ("Sense"). The *Vancouver Sun* began its story by quoting historian Michael Bliss: Clarkson is "a woman of grace, intelligence, and culture. She had become a very distinguished Canadian through something other than politics" (Greenaway and Bryden). The *Calgary Herald*'s Lawrence Martin rather ambiguously suggested that Clarkson had been attracted to the position because of its "status" ("But Watch").

The *National Post*'s Mark Steyn, referring sarcastically to Clarkson's reputation for refinement and arrogance, called her "good Queen Adrienne" and suggested that she and her longtime companion and newly acquired husband, writer John Ralston Saul, would benefit Canada by even looking like Queen Elizabeth and Prince Philip: "And don't they seem sorta like Royal lookalikes, anyway? Adrienne the round-faced Queen in her Windsor perm and John the lanky, balding Duke of Edinburgh with his penchant for 'controversial' interventions. Granted, they're not particularly good Royal lookalikes but, if you were booking a singing telegram in Sarnia for your mum's birthday, you'd be pretty impressed" ("Long Live Queen Adrienne"). Jan Wong of the *Globe and Mail* made a similar observation: "Adrienne Clarkson and her husband are body-doubles for Queen Elizabeth and Prince Philip. The gals have the same hairdo, the same odd fashion sense (kimonos and kilts). The guys have the same receding hairline, the same double-breasted fashion sense (grey suits and grey suits)" ("On Madame Clarkson").

The *Calgary Herald*'s Barry Cooper and David Bercuson, also sceptical of Clarkson's appropriateness, argued that her royal refinement was of the wrong kind for the job and hinted that it was inauthentic: "The office is properly one of form, dignity, and gravity opposed precisely to that exquisitely refined but fashionably left-wing *snobisme* characteristic of people with an overdeveloped sense of self-importance."

Michael Valpy expressed slightly different misgivings. "Ms. Clarkson," he suggested, "will lean a little heavily towards ceremony and grandeur." Alliance Party MP Deborah Grey quipped that she was "almost wondering how the Queen will feel about curtseying" to Clarkson (Mulawka). In an article oozing with the writer's class, gender, and regional biases and titled "The Lady Oughta Zip Her Lip: GG Clarkson out of Line with Haughty Sermons," *Winnipeg Sun* columnist Ross McLennan declared her "pseudo-queen Adrienne," "our counterfeit queen," "a synthetic blue blood," "her royal Drone Clone," and "her Mock Majesty." McLennan continued: "'We are initiating the holding of a public levee in each province and territory we visit,' she declared. 'You are all invited.' It's as if Marie Antoinette decided to put Versailles on wheels and trundle it before mouth-gaping peasants across the length and breadth of France." McLennan's comparison of Clarkson to Marie Antoinette—whom he implicitly condemned while making the comparison—suggested what he might like to see done to her.

Robert Fife of the *National Post* wrote a humorously under-stated article about a new painting by Ken Lochhead, "in which the couple are depicted as seventeenth-century royalty." He also quoted Lochhead as saying, "If they are going to be glamorous and have panache, I thought I'd put them in some outfits that are fitting the occasion" ("Your Very Own"). With the article, the *Post* published a photo of the painting, which depicted Clarkson and Saul looking blissfully happy in powdered wigs and billows of lace.

Also in the *National Post,* Scott Feschuk created a mock interview with Clarkson. In it, Clarkson objected to the term "vice-regal," because "it makes the whole thing sound so half-assed," and explained that one of her qualifications for the position was that she was so used to hearing people say "excellency" to her that she would "instinctively turn and look right down at them." However, the *Post* also commissioned COMPAS Research to conduct a public opinion poll on the appointment, the results of which it partially released in mid-October. The full October 5, 1999 COMPAS report to the *Post* stated that eighty-three percent of Canadians judged Clarkson's appointment to be either "good" (sixty-five percent) or "very good" (eighteen percent). A Gallup poll released around the same time indicated that support for the monarchy had risen eight percent since Clarkson's appointment (Farley).

A small number of editorials and articles—in several newspapers, among them the *Toronto Star* and the *Globe and Mail*—reflected on the possibility of doing away with the monarchy altogether and establishing an entirely Canadian head of state. In a sense, this would be a logical outcome of the seemingly paradoxical focus on Canadian nationalism and royalty in the various responses to Clarkson.

In these responses, Clarkson's image as an appropriate national symbol had been supported by two factors. The first was her association with some of the country's national institutions: the CBC, McClelland and Stewart, Canadian literature, bilingualism, and multiculturalism. Mixed in with this were Clarkson's well-known politically nationalist opinions on free trade and state-supported culture. The second factor was the way her personal history as a refugee and immigrant from Asia appeared to symbolize Canada's changing racial and ethnic makeup.

Her image as suitably (or unsuitably) "royal" has been supported by the connections between various Canadian national institutions and her personal life story. She was a refugee and immigrant who had steadily ascended the social ladder and could plausibly reach the highest rung. Her ascent had taken her through a number of Canadian institutions, many of them associated with high culture—Trinity College, CBC cultural affairs broadcasting (which embraced ballerinas and opera singers and Renaissance painters), and the Canadian Museum of Civilization. All her quasi-royal qualities were Canadian ones—defined, produced, and enacted in Canada. "My education, my formation, all the important influences outside my emotional childhood world were through Canadian public institutions," she told Maggie Farley of the *Los Angeles Times*. "So there's no accident about the fact that I now really kind of represent it." It was easy for Clarkson's supporters and her detractors to believe that she was about as "royal" a person as Canada could produce. And it was easy for her.

TAKE THREE

Viceregal Ex-Novelists

OR: Imaginary Autobiographies
Some Culture More Condoling

I can share some of the queen's social pieties and admire her mother's World War II bravery while still lamenting the social cost of monarchy. And of other would-be aristocracies. When I was a boy soprano, one of my recital songs was the Cavalier lyric "Boot, Saddle, to Horse and Away." I still like the melody. My grade six class painted a mural of the Battle of Hastings; I drew the duke's Viking ships. Funny how the notion of "royal" gets linked to wanderers and boat people. I, too, once wandered off to Britain and France, but much later than Adrienne Clarkson did. A few times, I saw Prince Rainier stop at the Col de Villefranche and send his chauffeur into my local tabac to buy a paper. I don't think royalty explains much, but maybe more conventional fiction will.

Now, Clarkson is not only semiroyal, but she was also once a writer like me. Well, not quite like me. There have been a few semiroyal novelists—Madame de Stael, Lord Bulwer-Lytton, Lord Archer. Demi-semiroyal. In grade six, when I wasn't having fantasies about being an adventurous writer, I had sex fantasies about either Princess Margaret or Rhonda Fleming.

In three weeks, I've been able to buy all of John Ralston Saul's novels on eBay. For a few American dollars. Fantasies don't always make one a royalist. Copies of Clarkson's novels seem to exist nowhere except in libraries. The very few reviews of them that I can find say they are populated by aristocrats and Influential People. Reviews of Saul's novels often mention beautiful young Chinese women. Perhaps both Clarkson and Saul were both looking ahead. "Fairy tales can come true, / It can happen to you"—that was a big song back in 1955. I once read *The Last Days of Pompeii*, but few people read it anymore either.

Sex has become the most successful bull market of the last three decades. (John Ralston Saul, *The Doubter's Companion* 266)

My novels written years ago are perfectly forgettable,
With characters and plots that are embarrassingly juvenile.
With heroes and my heroines named Raoul Gretchen and
    Tiercel
Still nothing as far-fetched as my becoming Governor
    General. (Stephen Lautens)

Along with her unfortunate alienation from her daughters and her last-minute marriage to Saul, Adrienne Clarkson's two long-forgotten novels became an inviting target for her critics in the days following her appointment. Critics wary of challenging her credentials for the position but sensing a demonstrable failure in her distant past retrieved the novels from public libraries and read them for the first time.

Jonathon Gatehouse, for example, reported in the *National Post* that the novels were out of print, "but a search through Toronto public library archives yesterday suggests her career change may have been a wise decision." He went on to quote two of the novels' more sententious passages. A month later, Frank Moher, also in the *Post,* declared that the "waters of obscurity have closed over the two novels," and Clarkson "has done us all a favour by attempting to leave them there. The *National Post,* however, has no such scruples"—which, of course, Moher's colleague Gatehouse had already demonstrated. He went on to ridicule the characters' names, their interest in Shakespeare, and their habit of speaking "in semicolons." He also misread the novels' criticism of anti-Semitism as an example of it and argued that their portrayal of Canada as "second rate" in comparison to Europe was part of a plot to get government money to pour "into things like arts and culture."

Clarkson's *A Lover More Condoling* (1968) and *Hunger Trace* (1970) are among the earliest novels written by a Chinese-Canadian author, although they have rarely been listed as such and are not noted in Lien Chao's survey of Chinese-Canadian writing, *Beyond Silence* (1997). This may be because Clarkson has so strongly affiliated herself with the much larger white, anglophone community. It could also be explained by the fact that there is nothing overtly Chinese about the setting, characters, or form of the novels. Clarkson has said that they were written approximately eight years apart, which makes *A Lover More*

Condoling a work of the early 1960s and suggests that its publication was facilitated by her sudden celebrity as *Take 30* co-host. She has also insisted several times that neither novel is the least bit autobiographical. In 1968, she stated, "Novels are not a form of autobiographic art. They're not a vehicle for the artist to tell you why he was severely toilet trained. They're an adventure of the imagination. If you want a cool lucid biography, read Bertrand Russell" (McCracken).

The declaration is so emphatic and unreasonable (there have been many fine semi-autobiographical novels, including Margaret Laurence's *The Diviners,* published the year before McCracken's interview), and its terms so exaggeratedly opposed ("toilet training" versus "lucid"), that a reader could be forgiven for suspecting there is considerable Clarkson autobiography—or autobiographical desire—in her fiction. And, of course, whatever a person writes reflects her interests and knowledge, and to some extent her attitudes and assumptions.

Both novels have at least an indirect connection to Clarkson's life. Both contain many references to France, where Clarkson has lived for extended periods. Both promote the idea that we should focus on culture, and the search for beauty and pleasure, before material security and career. In this way, they reflect Clarkson's attempts to turn the attention of Canadians towards the arts in television series such as *Adrienne Clarkson's Summer Festival* and *Adrienne Clarkson Presents.* The protagonists of the two novels— schoolteacher Sara Rainer of *A Lover More Condoling,* and the itinerant, self-educated Regina Adler of *Hunger Trace*—incessantly quote the major English poets like enthusiastic recent graduates of a first-year college-English survey. This, too, is reflected in their author's life: Clarkson often employs literary quotations, and her sources are usually limited to the standard works of

British and Canadian writing. Both Sara and Regina are sexually attracted to tall, slender men; the descriptions of these men eerily echo newspaper descriptions of Clarkson's two husbands. Both novels implicitly insist on acceptance of sexual and racial difference; heterosexual and homosexual characters get along easily in each. Both link the puritan fear of adventure, beauty, and the unknown with anti-Semitism. Both novels are also built on literary stereotypes: France is cultured, European art is beautiful, rural Canada is culturally impoverished, heterosexual men are aggressive, homosexual men are graceful and artistic, art is spiritually uplifting, travel is broadening, women are generally passive. Such stereotypes also appear in Clarkson's journalism and in speeches she has given as governor general.

Together with the novels of John Ralston Saul, Clarkson's novels represent the two stereotypical poles of male- and female-authored popular fiction in contemporary North America. Clarkson's main characters are women; Saul's are men. Her main characters seek love and beauty; his seek money, power, sexual confirmation, and adventure. Her actions unfold in the private world of domestic relations; his unfold in the public worlds of military intrigue, political corruption, and commercial greed. Both authors portray men as active, scheming, and achievement-seeking while portraying women as passive, accepting, and more curious about what may happen than hopeful of influencing it. The dominant images of her novels are flowers, gardens, household interiors, and objets d'art; those of his are guns, jungles, drugs, office buildings, and money.

By genre, his novels are male adventure quests; hers are somewhat modified Harlequin romances. Margaret Atwood prefaces her 1981 novel *Bodily Harm* with an epigraph from John Berger: "A man's presence suggests what he is capable of doing to you or for you. By contrast, a woman's presence . . . defines what can and cannot be done to her." While *Bodily Harm* challenges the world Berger describes, Clarkson's and Saul's novels assume and affirm that polarization of the sexes. Men act, and women watch men act—usually with fear or admiration in Saul, and with detachment or bemusement in Clarkson. Both Saul and Clarkson are also less interested in how their characters came to hold such gendered views than in narrating the adventures that ensue from them. Their novels neither critique gender assumptions nor attempt psychological depth. But while Saul's were presented unashamedly as potboilers and were largely accepted as such by reviewers, Clarkson's, with their many allusions to art and litera-ture, were presented as serious literature and were accorded little attention by reviewers.

A Lover More Condoling focuses on Sara Rainer, a thirty-nine-year-old widow who has had no romantic life since the demise of her young soldier-husband. He suffered an absurd death shortly after their marriage, nineteen years before, during the D-Day landings. In fact, Sara has never had a romantic life. Her marriage to Norman (most likely Clarkson was punning on "norm man") was merely a commonsense arrangement with a decent young man who fulfilled her practical, small-town Ontario aspirations. At the opening of the novel, Sara is in France. She has travelled there reluctantly in order to help dedicate a memo-rial to her husband, and she finds the place unpleasant and "confusing," despite the presence of her Canadian friend Diana, a longtime resident. Procrastinating about proceeding on to Normandy, Sara rents a house in a small village south of Paris. There, she encounters a wealthy, mysterious, and worldly painter, Guy, who repeatedly enters her house uninvited, and who is determined to melt her diffidence about romance. He's also bent on seducing her.

The situation is saturated with coincidence and stereotype. The painter just happens to be estranged from his wife, and he just happens to live in the house next door, which allows the action of the novel to be facilitated by the back gate that connects the two properties. The village just happens to contain an abandoned medieval church, which the novelist can use as the Gothic site for part of her protagonist's transformation. Sara is the stereotypical sexually repressed, Protestant Canadian ice maiden. This is the same stereotype lamented by Irving Layton, memorably evoked by Sinclair Ross with Mrs. Bentley and by Margaret Laurence with Hagar Shipley, and institutionalized as a national treasure by Margaret Atwood in *Survival.*

Sara is also the innocent young middle-class woman of the classic Gothic novel who strays into aristocratic society as a governess or nurse and has baffling encounters with men who may be either suitors or sexual predators. Guy is more than just another guy (although he is that too): he's the ambiguously attractive and potentially dangerous Gothic hero. Their relationship also echoes the transatlantic encounters between North American naivety and European experience that constitute most of Henry James's novels. In Clarkson's novel, as in James's works, North America is a place of crassness, unimaginative practicality, and fear of risk, adventure, and passion. Europe is, in contrast, a place of near decadence where the world-weary sophistication of the beautiful Alienor de Lisse Bosquet, Guy's mistress, can earn her forgiveness for having collaborated with the Third Reich. It's also a place where "adultery" or "fornication"—terms a North American might use—are regarded as signs of social grace, or an appreciation of beauty, or an awareness that in this finite and fallen world one must seize whatever pleasure one can. Sara, the novel tells us, has allowed herself to procrastinate in life, to be passive and unadventurous, by imagining that her possibilities will remain unbounded. Guy mocks her: "That life is free and limitless is a luxury only faithful widows can allow themselves" (100).

A Lover More Condoling consists of several chapters of flirtation, foreplay, and discussions of rape, which are eventually resolved by two flaccid scenes of intercourse. (The concept that heterosexual mating is a kindly woman allowing a needy man to have a weak orgasm inside her curiously influences both of Clarkson's novels.) The foreplay begins with Guy's first appearance, when he taunts Sara for coming from a provincial Canadian culture that is "pure and tight" (21). It continues in their second meeting, when he tells her that she looks "so prim and prunes" and suggests that she "Give in, just a little." It becomes symbolically sexual on their third meeting, when he enters her house unannounced while her sister and brother-in-law are visiting. Sara finds Guy in the kitchen, "standing over the stove, lighting his cigarette from one of the burners . . . She motioned him with her hand to get out by the back door, almost as if he were a burglar and she was the housemaid-turned-accomplice. He smiled and shifted his weight to the other foot, giving the impression that he was even more firmly planted beside the stove. Sara did not know what she could do short of pushing him out" (33).

This kind of obvious Freudian imagery runs through the book. Here, Guy forces his way into the house that symbolizes Sara's body, lights his "cigarette" from one of her "burners," while she attempts to "push him out." In another scene, when he insists that she eat a bowl of soup that he has prepared for her, Sara responds sarcastically but unknowingly, "Eat me" (66).

The scene in which Guy cheerfully considers raping her begins with Sara becoming proudly aware of the Jamesian cultural differences between them. As he embraces her, "she could feel herself disliking him and not wanting to hear about his life; the peregrinations of rich people—their easy access to objects and their easy escape from them—repelled her . . . Sara stood there with his arms around her and tried to think of the taste of cold spring water at Gran's house where the pump had stood outside the back door until just three years ago. She felt Guy shift behind her, and she leaned back against him deliberately; the distinctness of his lips against hers gave her something to concentrate on, and she could feel herself focussing until she heard herself saying no. He gripped her hair on either side of her head above the ears and shook her gently, 'Why the hell not, you silly bitch?'" (112).

Despite the controlled violence of Guy's words, the narrative remains cheerful; when Sara answers, "Because," we are told that "they both began to laugh together." Continuing this paradoxical tone of affectionate violence, Guy deplores what he sees as Sara's childlike view of human affection: "Oh Sara, dear infuriating woman, will I eventually have to rape you?" When she banteringly replies, "you could have me drugged, have your way," he counters by teasing that she is too "Canadian" to be rapable: "You could probably fight me successfully, full of all that Canadian wheat germ and Girl Scout training. And think of the remorse. After all, *chérie,* I think rape is only for virgins. If I thought it would shock you, I would do it . . . " (112–13).

Throughout this scene, and elsewhere in the novel, the critical focus of the narrative is not on Guy and his concept of benign rape, but on Sara. She is too critical, the novel implies, too rigid, insufficiently hedonistic, and too ungiving. It is not good to be a virgin, whether an actual one or a virtual one—as Sara is, because of her nineteen years of celibate widowhood. Indeed, rape might do her good, the narrative implies, as its focus narrows abruptly to her ungivingness. Guy asks, "'Love me a little, Sara.' She shook her head rapidly, and felt alarming tears coming to her eyes. 'No, no, I don't know what you want from me. I don't know what you want. Don't hold me, please'" (113). The rapidity of Sara's refusal, and the array of negatives in her speech (two of them doubled), mark her as overdetermined and irrational and show Guy, the would-be rapist, to be the more reasonable and affectionate.

The conclusion of the novel confirms this interpretation of Sara. Throughout the action, a minor character, an abject homosexual called Amory, lurks on the fringes of the novel's action. Amory once tried to have a heterosexual relationship with Sara's friend Diana, and Diana—in Sara's view—cruelly discarded him. Diana visits Sara at her village house, and Amory also shows up. He is hoping, unrealistically, for a chance to renew their affair while also beginning a dalliance with Sara's sister, Anne. Finding herself alone with Amory, Sara wants to "say something to him about Anne, to say don't break her heart with your gentleness, your wistfulness, your magnificent ineptitude for life." Instead, she inexplicably reveals to him that she has dreamed of him recently. When he says, "Sara, you've always been so kind to me," she finds herself letting him make love to her and then comforting him afterwards—"She stroked his head absent-mindedly . . . The poor man, she thought, the poor man" (127).

Less than twenty hours later, Sara is in bed, wrapped in bandages. She has suffered extensive yet superficial burns as the result of having accidentally set off fireworks in the ruined church while she, Diana, Guy, Anne, Amory, and several others are presenting an avant-garde reading of *A Midsummer's Night's Dream*. Visited by the perennially amorous Guy, she says, "Oh, Guy, don't. It's not fair. I'm all bandaged." The long-mooted rape scene ensues, in a lighthearted manner, similar to the one in which it was first considered. "'I'm protesting with my poor bandaged arms, aren't you sorry for me.' He lifted his head and hissed, 'No-o-o-o.' Then it was over. I wonder how much time that took, she thought, as he slid to her side. Why did I make all that fuss about it, she thought as she stared at the back of his head . . ." (154).

A page later, Sara reflects that "my wanting you and my not wanting you; they were two sides of the same thing." Before she can reflect further, a drunken friend, also injured in the fireworks explosion, reels into the room and collapses on the bed beside Guy. Next come Sara's middle-class landlady and the mayor and the priest of the Normandy town in which her husband died. The novel ends with laughter, the mayor's pompous address to the faithful Canadian widow, and farce.

Overall, *A Lover More Condoling* is an odd novel. It reflects a variety of interests that do not always go well together. It certainly reflects Clarkson's francophilia, as well as her view that Canada and Canadians need to be more welcoming to art and less utilitarian in their outlook. It suggests that Europe, and France in particular, has a cultural richness that could enrich Canadians as well, but it also symbolizes that richness in starkly sexual terms. Art, culture, imagination, and sexual adventure are tightly entwined. Sara's passive celibacy stands as a symbol for Canadian puritanism, pragmatism, and lack of interest in art, culture, and adventure. Amory's sexual ambiguity signals his humanity and his openness to the possibilities of the world. Guy's rich sexual life with his estranged wife, his mistress, and Sara, combined with his wit and his proficiency as a painter, suggest that his commitment to the beautiful moment is superior to the goal-oriented, risk-avoiding behaviour of most of the Canadian characters. When Sara lies in bed reflecting that she has opened herself to the ejaculate of "two men in twenty-four hours," Clarkson has her add: "And I haven't even had a bath in between; perhaps that's why the French have bidets. By their deeds you shall know them, she thought to herself and giggled" (155).

The implication is clearly that French women need bidets because they have a better attitude towards sexual relations than do the women of Sara's Protestant, Bible-quoting culture. Her "By their deeds you shall know them" is a popular misrendering of Matthew 7:20, part of Christ's Sermon on the Mount, and it implies that Sara's Canadian puritanism is a folk puritanism rather than a genuine appreciation of Christ's teachings. ("By their fruits ye shall know them," Christ says in the King James translation, speaking of the narrowly doctrinaire Jewish Pharisees whom he would criticize in Matthew 7:16 after declaring, "Ye shall know them by their fruits. Do men gather grapes of thorns or figs of thistles?")

The novel also implies here and elsewhere a fascination with the bohemian—with its impulsiveness and its sense of life as farce. The reader can get the impression that both author and protagonist are enjoying a little sex tourism; that by setting the novel in France, Clarkson is allowing both herself and Sara possibilities that were unavailable to them in Canada. Still, the narrow, masculinist tone of two of the novel's three reviews suggest that such tourism may have been necessary in Canada circa 1968. In the *University of Toronto Quarterly*, Gordon Roper called the novel a "confection . . . written with spirit and sparkle." H.T.K. (H.T.

Kirkwood), the *Canadian Forum* reviewer, found the story improbable and "weightless" and suggested that "perhaps it was intended to be." He liked Clarkson's characterization of Guy, whom he called a "robust free-wheeler," but he added the sexist and homophobic comment that the novel's "world of women with scarcely the shadow of a child and with only one real man among their numerous fairy good friends, is unreal." In *Saturday Night,* Jack Batten offered a similar homophobic appraisal—but of Guy: "the elegant, gallant fellow who is the widow's chief pursuer comes across as a raging faggot." Catherine Breslin, writing her profile of Clarkson a year after the novel's publication, offered a slightly less inflammatory appraisal, calling it "a lugubrious tale of a priggy Canadian widow learning the art of decadence in France."

Her second novel, *Hunger Trace,* which Clarkson says she wrote during her period of excitement at having her first novel published, is about a young woman who, at first glance, seems utterly different from Sara Rainer. Regina Adler is half-Jewish, a fact that her puritan Canadian mother concealed from her throughout most of her childhood. At the age of thirty-two, Regina has few, if any, sexual inhibitions or anxieties, and since her adolescence she has happily slept with any man who attracts her and "asks nicely." Supporting herself by taking the occasional job, often as a fashion model, she lives independently and itinerantly, spending much of her time in Europe.

Yet Regina's commitment to life as a free spirit arises from her rejection of the same puritan attitudes that constrain Sara, and on the same puritan-Canada/libertine-France dichotomy that Sara encounters in her French village. Regina's maternal family, the Hobbses, descended from an Anglican bishop; they are an upper-middle-class product of the puritan emphasis on propriety, caution, and materialism that dominated the rural culture in which Regina grew up. "The inside of jars of dried apricots and prunes, mingled with black Melton-cloth winter coats in moth-balls was the essence of Hobbses," Regina sarcastically recalls (76). Regina's escape from this world is through her father, a Jewish refugee who repeatedly disappointed and scandalized Regina's mother with his irregular business ventures and by keeping and training a large falcon. At seventeen, Regina flees to Paris to her father's aunt, her great-aunt Valancy Wertheim, an elderly lesbian poet and novelist who, when young, "ran off with a woman painter and they lived happily in Italy for a while and many women fell madly in love with her, and men too" (97). Aunt Valancy's flat on the rue du Bac near the Sorbonne is a dusty, jumbled museum of rare books and modernist artworks, many of them gifts from lovers or suitors. Aunt Valancy teaches Regina not only to appreciate poetry but also to live, as she has, "dangerously: it is only the careful drivers, she said, who have accidents" (104).

Hunger Trace thus situates Regina symbolically between the "rude country" of Canada, where people bravely endure unhappy marriages and take pride in their sensible clothes, respectable Rosedale homes, and white Protestant heritage, and France, where sensitivity and gallantry are prized and where Aunt Valancy lives impetuously and irregularly. Invited to a Rosedale home, Regina delights in teasing the prim housewives she meets there with the image of her unconventional aunt: "Betty asked, 'She never married?' thinking, I'm sure: embittered old maid." Regina answers, "'Oh yes, but she went on to other things; she stole the hearts of some of the loveliest ladies in Paris.'" To this, the housewives respond, "'Ladies!' . . . their Upper-Canadian anxiety showing through," as Regina had hoped it would (126).

As she did in *A Lover More Condoling,* Clarkson stages a collision between a staid, homogenous Canada and a disturbing European other. In each novel, the "otherness" of Europeans is based in part on their attachment to art and culture, and in part on their acceptance of homosexuality. What Clarkson adds in *Hunger Trace,* however, is the otherness of ethnicity—the Jewishness of Regina's father and Aunt Valancy. Despite having married a Jew, Regina's "Upper-Canadian" mother is, according to her daughter, a confirmed anti-Semite: "She always calls anyone who cheats her 'a little Hebrew'" (83). Jewishness here is aligned, in contrast to puritanism, with the ability to experience pleasure and to appreciate art, as well as with "a concern for the uncommercial" (39).

Yet the action of *Hunger Trace* suggests that a collision of these worlds—those of the puritan and the free spirit—may be disastrous. Free-living Regina begins a casual affair with ageing but affable patrician businessman Gratton Fairfield, "scion of the Hamilton Fairfields." Gratton is "full of decency and fair play and never forgets Mother's Day," and his father's company retains a suite at Toronto's fashionable King Edward Hotel (33). Within days of starting this affair, Regina becomes attracted to Senator Tiercel Margrave, a respected stockbroker and decorated World War II pilot, who is a close friend of Fairfield and who wants to arrange for Fairfield's nomination as a Liberal Party candidate in the next provincial election. Very soon, Regina is having affairs with both men while being hosted by their Rosedale wives. Although she breaks it off with Fairfield, his political opponents learn about their affair. This prevents his nomination and ruins Margrave's reputation as a "fixer" within the Liberal Party.

Two other ethnic characters besides the half-Jewish Regina also have negative effects on these Canadian aristocratic lives. One is

Gratton Fairfield's chief rival for the Liberal nomination, whom Senator Margrave describes as "a scab," and to whom Clarkson gives the Hungarian name of Szabo (81). The senator has been scheming for years to crush this man, and he considers himself politically cuckolded when Szabo learns of Fairfield's indiscretion and threatens to go public with it unless Fairfield withdraws his candidacy. The second such ethnic character is Gaetan, an inmate of a halfway house operated by the senator's do-gooder brother, Peregrine, an Anglican reverend. Peregrine describes Gaetan as "a quarter Indian, but mainly French-Canadian, with some Scottish thrown in; he's been up for armed robbery and got a bullet in his skull, which makes him rather slow and he prefers to speak French, although he used to speak English" (59).

One of the Margrave family's charitable works is taking the halfway house inmates on outings. The senator's eight-year old daughter, Gretchen, and Regina (invited because she speaks French) go along on several of these outings, and Gaetan, appearing gentle and confused, becomes fond of both of them. On the day the senator learns that Regina has unwittingly ruined his political reputation, Gaetan abducts Gretchen. When the child becomes restless and unhappy, he kills her. Despairing and drunk, the senator kills himself by crashing his private plane.

The novel is crude in several ways. The coincidence of Gretchen's abduction and Szabo's treachery happening almost concurrently creates an extremely contrived ending. The fact that both the villainous Szabo and the child-killing Gaetan are not Anglo-Saxon produces a strong scent of ethnic and racial stereotyping. The contrast between the sober, public-minded, excessively "decent," and quietly arrogant Upper Canadians such as the Margraves, the Hobbses, and the Fairfields on the one hand, and the art- and freedom-loving Regina and Aunt Valancy on the other is so severely drawn that both sets of characters often seem to be parodies. The Harlequin-romance pairing of Regina, naive about politics and social power, and Senator Tiercel Margrave, who is alternatively sensitive, ruthless, considerate, and cynical, is more subtle than that of Sara and Guy in *A Lover More Condoling,* yet it's still more clichéd than convincing. Most limiting is Clarkson's handling of Regina's first-person narration. Perhaps because of the polarizations in the narrative— male/female, puritan/bohemian, duty/pleasure, public/personal, Christian/Jewish, critical/generous, Canadian/European—which prompt arguments in which only one position is endorsed, Clarkson is unable to demonstrate clearly Regina's reliability as a narrator. Most of the time, Regina is associated with the preferred position—personal, female, artistic, generous, European—which makes her narrative seem trustworthy, as when she is skewering her mother's anti-Semitism, or celebrating her Aunt Valancy's insouciant independence. But at other times, her judgement seems suspect, particularly when it comes to the senator; she seems oblivious to his heavy drinking and unconcerned about his callous manipulation of his fellow politicos or his WASP arrogance towards Szabo.

Also awkward, and somewhat confusing, is the falcon imagery that dominates much of the book. Calliope, the falcon kept by Regina's father, appears to represent his nonpuritan impracticality and his awareness of the savage passions that lie beneath both bourgeois pretension and high European culture. The falcon also hints at the savagery of "cultured" Third Reich Germany. As well, the senator and his brother are named after falcons—Tiercel and Peregrine—and the senator flies a private plane that, in an allusion to the high-flying French author Saint-Exupéry, he calls *Petit Prince.* Regina explains the novel's title, *Hunger Trace,* as a line that forms across the claws and feathers of a bird that "goes without regular feeding for only a day . . . not a line exactly but a weakness in each claw and feather. When the feathers and claws grow out to that point, they have to break. For . . . a bird of prey like a falcon or any hawk, it means they can't hunt for a while" (74). Indeed, when Regina takes poorly fed Calliope out for a practice hunt, the bird is unable to dive with accuracy.

This imagery seems to suggest that the senator himself is a bird of prey who feeds off the lesser politicians whose careers he manipulates and often ruins. He's prevented from "feeding" when Regina undermines his plans for Gratton Fairfield. He loses control of his life and plunges, like an out-of-condition falcon, to his death. His death plunge is clearly presented as parallel to Calliope's failed dive. One difficulty with this imagery is that it nullifies Gretchen's murder as a motivation for his apparent suicide, making it unnecessary to the novel. Another is that by using the image in the novel's title, the author designates the senator as the central character, which he clearly is not. Narrator Regina Adler, who is not rapacious, who refuses to accompany the senator on his final flight, and who does not fail in any of her own flights of adventure, is the novel's main character.

Like *A Lover More Condoling, Hunger Trace* can easily be read as reflecting aspects of Clarkson's life. She was living in Rosedale when she wrote her second novel. Her husband, Stephen Clarkson, had recently run as a Liberal candidate for mayor of Toronto and—as Gratton Fairfield had hoped to do—for a seat in the Ontario Legislature. Both Clarksons had been active in the Liberal Party and undoubtedly had dealings with Liberal senators, fixers, and bagmen similar to those Clarkson depicts in the novel. Gratton Fairfield himself, with the Hamilton Fairfield family fortune behind him, bears some resemblance to Stephen Clarkson, to whom the Clarkson Gordon family fortune lent credibility and influence. The Rosedale drawing rooms inhabited by idle matrons, in which much of the novels' action is set, would also have been known to Clarkson.

More significant, however, is the coding of otherness as disruption in the novel. In the absence of Chinese characters, Jewishness serves as a symbol of racial difference. Regina is troubled by her half-Jewishness and by how the banality and materialism of white Anglo-Saxon Canadian culture have increased her desire to identify with the Jewish part of her heritage. But her mother and her sister, Alta, insist on concealing it. When Regina's father (who, like Clarkson's own father, is an Anglican) attempts to provoke her mother by asking to be buried as a Jew, she is scandalized and tries to enlist her daughters in her efforts to resist the request. Alta exclaims that it would "kill" her husband's business "if anyone suspected, even suspected, a Jewish connection" (227).

Regina is also troubled that even her Aunt Valancy has seemed embarrassed by her own Jewishness and has tried to pass as a non-Jew. The passage in which she asks her aunt about this is especially arresting: "Once . . . I asked her about her family and my father's, and it was then I learned that they had been converted Jews for two generations before her and therefore, she delicately pointed out, could not be considered to be Jews of the ghetto; I told her that my mother had only told me when I was fully grown about the Wertheims and the Adlers and she shrugged and said enigmatically that there were some things that only one's mother should tell you. It sounded false, and Aunt Valancy rarely said anything false, even for effect—brittle, tautological, harsh, but never false. It gave me an idea of the depth of discomfort that being Jewish caused her, even though she was beautiful, loved, and clever; even though she disguised it so well, and spoke of it so eloquently and so charmingly" (184–85).

It is tempting to read this passage as Clarkson commenting indirectly on herself—a member of a family that "converted" several generations back to Christianity, "beautiful, loved, and clever," able to speak "eloquently and charmingly," able to disguise her difference "so well," yet always, indisputably and unforgettably, nonwhite.

John Ralston's Saul's first published book might not have been a novel had his 653-page doctoral thesis—"The Evolution of Civil-Military Relations in France After the Algerian War" (King's College, London, 1975)—been more positively received by his academic supervisors. John Lownsbrough, quoting Saul in 1993, characterized Saul's relationship with his supervisors as a "contest of wills": "'They disagreed with my thesis,' remembers Saul indignantly, 'but what bothered them was that since my sources were the most impeccable primary sources, they couldn't refute my thesis unless they discredited my sources.'" He did get his degree, though.

Saul was eager to expand his thesis and publish at least some of it in France, especially the parts that concerned the mysterious death of President Charles de Gaulle's chief of staff, General Ailleret, in an unexplained March 1968 plane crash on the Indian Ocean island of Réunion. But Saul thought that this might not be possible. He explained to Barbara Amiel, "Under French law, a nonfiction book on French politics by a foreigner can be seized by the Minister of the Interior and confiscated without recourse to the courts. Why research for six years only to have your book gather dust?" As a result of these concerns, Saul wrote a semi-fictionalized narrative of his process of research and published a French version in Paris in the spring of 1977 as *Mort d'un Général*; six months later, a Toronto publisher issued an English version under the title *The Birds of Prey*. The novel's thesis—that General Ailleret was murdered by a right-wing officer clique descended from the collaborationist army of Vichy France, a clique still dominant within the French government—was understandably provocative to the French. In its various editions (none of which were published in the U.S.), the novel eventually sold more than a million copies.

In the French version, Saul's accusations were thinly veiled behind the pseudonyms assigned to the major players, including Ailleret—pseudonyms presumably insisted upon by a publisher nervous about being sued for libel. But in the English version, Ailleret was named. Perhaps as a result, most of the book's Canadian reviewers treated Saul's theory—that French army senior staff murdered Ailleret and the seventeen others aboard his DC-6 by sabotaging the plane as an explicit accusation.

In interviews, Saul has claimed some autobiographical relationship to the novel's protagonist: amateur historian, political scientist, and sleuth Charles Stone (see Inness). He's also said that many of the threats Stone receives during his investigation parallel threats he received himself while researching his thesis. "During his research on *l'affaire* Ailleret," Lownsbrough writes, "Saul got some not-so-veiled threats from government higher-ups, and suspects that his phone was tapped." Paul Hornbeck interviewed Saul when the novel was published. He reported that Saul had told him that he'd "had his phone tapped, was threatened by a former government cabinet minister, and was often faced with an antagonistic silence from officials involved in the original inquest." In retrospect, such claims seem a little self-aggrandizing, and they were perhaps mainly intended as scandalous publicity. Saul travelled safely through France after the novel came out, and he lived there during Clarkson's term as Ontario's agent general. If the book's portrayal of murderous corruption within France's government and business classes was accurate rather than merely sensational, it's likely that this portrayal—even if it didn't put Saul in physical danger—would have made it difficult for Clarkson to build working relationships with French businesses or bureaucracies.

The novel does, however, roughly resemble Saul's own research project on the Ailleret case. Like Saul, Charles Stone becomes curious about the unlikely plane crash in which Ailleret died and about the apparent failure of the French military to investigate it. Also like Saul, he comes to believe that the World War II split between the liberal-democratic free French forces of General Charles de Gaulle and the fascist-nationalist Vichy military of General Henri-Philippe Pétain continued after the war. Furthermore, both Saul and Stone believe that Pétain's faction—despite its leader's conviction for treason and his death while serving a life sentence—quickly came to dominate the postwar army. This faction, according to Stone, led the 1967 rebellion by the military against de Gaulle, by then France's president, who was attempting to withdraw the French armed forces from Algeria. Ailleret, Saul and Stone theorize, was one of the few senior officers loyal to de Gaulle, and he was murdered by his fellow officers because he was about to bring them firmly under his control. Some of the early pages of the novel read as if they were lifted directly from Saul's doctoral thesis.

Saul's suggestions to interviewers that Stone is, to some extent, a fictionalized version of his own investigating self are revealing. The novel's narrator openly idealizes Stone. His first description of Stone portrays him, Canute-like, contemplating the power of the returning tide: "He was a tall man, finely cut, his shoulders broad but too clearly drawn to be heavy. One could sense his back, calm beneath a thick sweater, resigned in the sea, which engulfed him. He appeared a silent man" (14). Next, the narrator describes him at a dinner as "amusing, attractive, civilized . . . The impression he did leave was one of self-confidence; not in the aggressive manner of someone justifying himself, but in the calm, disinterested way of someone who was blissfully unaware of the word 'doubt'" (15–16).

A few pages later, the narrator offers this characterization: "Stone was a tall man . . . He was perfectly integrated. That was a peculiar characteristic, but very real. He appeared at home with himself. His strength was deceivingly hidden because his lines were smooth and clean as if he were slight. His character appeared in the same way, deceptively hiding in its own good balance. And yet his character, on closer examination, was more restrained than balanced. And so his stride became more carefully fitted to the ground, perfectly calm, restrained, scarcely appearing to disturb the world about him. He wore baggy light trousers which floated in the slight breeze and no shirt. His hair, just slightly too long, blew in a gentle disorder, like a baroque decoration on an immaculate form" (19–20).

The repetitions here of "tall," "perfectly," and "calm" add to the general portrayal of self-containment and self-confidence, which, when the action of the novel begins, and Stone is thwarted, followed, threatened, and assaulted, is demonstrated by his repeated resourcefulness and imperturbability.

As it is in Saul's later novels, the eroticism in *The Birds of Prey* is almost entirely focused on the attractiveness of male bodies and male athleticism. The narrator frequently regards Stone's body in a voyeuristic fashion: "Stone lay face down, naked, asleep . . . The fingers were long and finely drawn without being delicate" (29). In contrast, female characters, including Melanie, the "pretty" young widow of a member of General Ailleret's aircrew with whom Stone becomes sexually involved, are given only perfunctory descriptions by the narrator. As Stone is a stand-in for the author, his portrayal implies a fair amount of self-fascination on the part of the young J.R. Saul—there is an amusing degree of self-objectification, self-evaluation, self-parody, vanity, and at times erotic narcissism going on here.

Stone's portrayal as "civilized" and "self-confident" gestures to other ways in which the character resembles Saul. He has made solitary journeys to war-torn Kenya and Morocco. He is "comforted" by the "wrought-iron balustrade" of the eighteenth-century Paris mansion in which he rents a flat (28). He has a wide knowledge of literature and history, at one point quoting T.S. Eliot, Keats, and Lewis Carroll to Melanie and in turn recognizing her allusions to Hugo, Baudelaire, and Saint-John Perse. He has a keen knowledge of wines, and a sense of fashion that allows him to dress appropriately for any venue. To some extent, these attributes echo genre conventions of detective or adventure fiction, reminding us of impeccably suave and well-travelled protagonists like Lord Peter Wimsey, Hercule Poirot, and James Bond.

But attributes like these are also mentioned in descriptions of Saul published in the 1970s and 1980s. Leo Ryan of the *Globe and Mail* wrote that Saul was dressed "in a natty British style, with a carnation in his lapel." In *Maclean's*, Barbara Amiel reported that the "grey double-breasted suit jacket author John Ralston Saul wears is unbuttoned. From its breast pocket a white handkerchief is spilling out in a little fan of soft pleats. His face is pale, weak-chinned, with a high forehead—a countenance that would not have been out of place among the dandy-aesthetes in the Eton-Oxford axis of a Harold Acorn, Cyril Connolly, or Evelyn Waugh."

Margaret Cannon, writing about Saul for the *Globe* in 1986, said, "From his perfectly tailored suit and elegant manners to his impeccable Upper Canadian English, John Ralston Saul appears to be a card-carrying member of the Canadian elite." John Lownsbrough described the Saul of the 1970s thus: "An eye for fine tailoring and the raffish accessory, the snappy car (a Lancia Fulvia replaced the Riley), and a ground-floor apartment on the rue Jacob added to the impression of *savoir-faire*."

Saul's travels between 1975 and 1979—while he was working for Petro-Canada as a special presidential assistant—to the jungles of Southeast Asia and to Morocco and the Spanish Sahara, are also echoed in the characterization of Stone. When the novel opens, Stone has just returned to France from Morocco. He is carrying with him a copy of an essay he has published "on jungle warfare in Malaysia," a country he had visited during its independence struggles by attaching himself to a British "parachute company" (16).

Stone is also characterized as a "loner." Saul himself has often been called a loner because of his lack of institutional and professional affiliations, and his scorn for careful and systematic scholarship. Stone trusts no one to assist him in his research in the Ailleret mystery and reveals his findings only to Melanie and the London newspaperman whose willingness to publish his work might offer some protection should the general's killers capture him. For sex, he prefers casual affairs with women who are not interested in friendship. One of these, Odile, accuses him of being "a fool and a loner" (166).

His solitariness and his air of being eccentrically cultured connect Stone to the major (perhaps only) Saul theme: the inhumanity of corporate structures and the banality of technocrats—the people who work like small machines, doing a single repetitive task without ever becoming curious about the structures that task may serve. Right-wing technocrats steer France towards defeat by Germany in 1940, regain power over the government and the military after the war, and murder Ailleret and his crew. The huge apparatus of the technocrats, which encompasses major right-of-centre political parties, many businesspeople, numerous members of the civil service—including many of the police and much of the army—becomes Stone's adversary. These loosely linked people perform their jobs and enjoy their privileges without asking how the system they serve is maintained. This situation allows Saul extraordinary novelistic freedom. Being unconsciously and pragmatically evil, the members of the apparatus are capable of almost anything. In their pursuit of Stone, they require no motivation, no carefully prepared reality. Hired thugs can strike and then disappear with impunity. Knives, guns, and rifles materialize in their hands as required. Skill at blackmail, wiretapping, marksmanship, or martial arts are postulated by the author whenever needed. Amid such vast and corrupt institutional power, almost any action is credible.

Some critics have read the novel's conclusion as ironic. In it, Stone is killed, and we learn that the publication of his research has had virtually no impact on the enormous conspiracy that governs France. But it's not so much ironic as it is the logical outcome of such a one-sided conflict. However, the conclusion does reveal Saul as amusingly self-aggrandizing, because it suggests that he, as the novelist-researcher of the Ailleret affair, has also been a lonely hero, a Luke Skywalker without an empire or a princess, a man who has been as brave and as foolish as Stone. By having Stone killed, Saul implicitly boasts that he has also risked mortal danger. However, an even greater narrative irony lies in the fact that it is Melanie who kills Stone's killer and delivers Stone's story to the British publisher. In an almost zombie-like state, the passive woman aims and fires Stone's gun. The dum-dum bullets that Stone has prepared shred his assailant's body.

For a period of several years after the novel appeared, Saul published, or allowed to be published, various romantic photos of himself as a solitary adventurer—with the Polisario in the Sahara, with Shan tribal warlords in Burma. He carried a tropical adventurer's hat with him to interviews and photo ops, the implication being that here was the kind of man who could play a major role in the plots and counterplots of his own books. His next novel, *Baraka*, came out in 1983. It's the tale of a young executive for an American oil company who is assigned the task of covertly selling several tons of armaments abandoned by the U.S. in Vietnam. By doing so, he hopes to raise enough cash to pay for oil leases that the Vietnamese government is covertly granting. This story, as well, vaguely parallels Saul's own life. In the late 1970s, when he was a young Petro-Canada executive, Saul travelled to Vietnam to obtain oil leases.

Baraka articulates more forcefully the theme of conflict between independent, humanistic creativity and bureaucratic instrumentalism. Mechanistic rational analysis, which in *The Birds of Prey* was represented by the Vichy army and its pragmatic murders of Ailleret, Stone, and others, is here represented by the Harvard MBA degree. Creativity and humanity are represented by the ageing oilman James Moffett (whom some commentators believe was partly modelled on Saul's boss at Petro-Canada, Maurice Strong). The novel develops through Saul's staged conflict between these two views, a conflict in which "good" is defined by the MBA holders as something that advances one's career or increases the profitability of one's company and by the humanists as something that lifts the human spirit, results in a spectacular business coup, or is instinctually recognizable. Moffett reflects, "let the others dress like serial numbers to avoid attracting attention . . . he would continue to dress well. Let them mask their power in the mysteries of corporate structure, he would be happy to deal with his as the raw thing that it was. Let them eat tasteless, meaningless food, he would continue to please his stomach. Let them hire technocrats with computer minds, he would continue to hire generalists if his instincts told him they were right" (33).

However, whereas in *The Birds of Prey* the author invites readers to identify with Stone and root for him, there are no admirable characters in *Baraka*. The novel's lead character, Martin Laing, is a young American who, like Saul, has an arts degree from McGill University; he also has an MBA from Harvard. Laing is a nervous, unfriendly man whose instincts are to trust no one completely, not even his mentor, Moffett. He has muddled dreams about the dormant sexuality of his beautiful wife, Cosima, whose career as an architect is being stifled by the quiet masculinism of the New York firm that employs her. Moffett's career as a senior oil company executive is blocked by plodding younger MBA employees like Laing; his hope that Laing will become more adventurous and imaginative turns out to be misplaced. Moffett's marriage has developed into a relationship between strangers; Laing's threatens to do the same. Moffett eventually kills himself.

Laing's attempts to sell the abandoned U.S. arms quickly implicate him in a murder and then lead him to double-cross the Polisario guerrillas, who purchase the arms, and his old friend Anthony Smith, who has helped arrange the sale. Cosima, meanwhile, has seduced the overweight Smith, but she finds intercourse with him uninteresting. In this scene, the narrator curiously spends more time describing Smith's obesity and his uncircumcised penis than he does describing the body of the allegedly beautiful Cosima. This narrative focus on the male body is characteristic of most of the sex scenes in the novel. Cosima, married to Laing, lusted after by Moffett, and enjoyed by Smith, constitutes an unconscious sexual bridge between the three male friends, linking them homoerotically through their sharing of her body as they are linked through their business relationships. Uncomfortable in these relationships, unable to trust anyone or to think clearly under stress, Laing stupidly stays close to the weapons. He is trapped there by the Moroccan Air Force, which has come to destroy the cache—an action that Laing himself has arranged. Smith escapes back to southern Morocco, where he happily partakes of the cheap wine, food, and child prostitutes.

Again, Saul's characters are one-dimensional figures: Cosima, who is bored and vaguely feminist; Laing, who is nervous but unscrupulously ambitious; Moffett, whose alleged interest in art, culture, and adventurous thinking is without passion, and whose critique of the MBAs is weak; and Smith, who is amoral, somewhat lazy, overweight, and pleasure-seeking. The general impression the novel offers is of a Western world that has grown weary of its own philistinism and pragmatism, and of a planet where Moorish architecture alone preserves a balance of beauty and practicality. The novel also seems sympathetic towards child prostitution, and towards men—puzzled by newly feminist Western women—who find solace in the company of other men and in the sexual ministrations of prepubescent girls. Like the narrative of *The Birds of Prey,* the narrative of *Baraka* is mildly homoerotic in its focus on male action and male bodies and in its contrasting vagueness about female bodies.

In interviews he gave at this time, Saul rather pretentiously compared himself to such novelists of ideas as Ford Madox Ford, Graham Greene, André Malraux, and V.S. Naipaul; he also insisted that his books were being misread as mere "thrillers," because North American readers were unfamiliar with those writers. Apparently unhappy that his books were bringing him financial success but no respect as a literary artist, he started adding to this comparison an attack on the most widely respected twentieth-century fiction. He declaimed that it was a "scandal" that James Joyce, Philip Roth, and Saul Bellow had become literary giants, arguing that their status should be at best "marginal." Ford, Greene, Malraux, and Naipaul were the "mainstream," he announced petulantly to Margaret Cannon in 1986 (ironically, Cannon was the *Globe and Mail's* specialist in adventure and detective fiction), and "I'm in the mainstream."

After interviewing him in June 1988, Joel Yanofsky of the Montreal *Gazette* summarized Saul's literary views thus: "Western fiction has become self-indulgent and irrelevant. James Joyce is a wonderful writer but 'a literary cul-de-sac.' Saul Bellow is the best of a misguided bunch who are obsessed with their own private language, their 'little pain' . . . In France, Britain, and the U.S. the marginal has become mainstream and the mainstream has been dismissed out of hand by tenured professors. But the mainstream writers—here he includes Voltaire, Zola, and Greene—have advanced the cause of literature. It is a tradition Saul considers himself a part of."

To the *Globe*'s H.G. Kirchhoff, later in 1988, Saul said he objected to being called a writer of "thrillers" and declared, "The people who influenced me were people like Conrad, Zola, Malraux and Graham Greene. I don't really know what a 'thriller' is." He went on to compare his interest in contemporary business practices to Melville's interest in the nineteenth-century whaling industry before adding, "I'm not comparing myself to Melville." Putting the relative merits of the novelists whose work Saul invokes aside, Saul's claim to be comparable to Greene or Malraux founders on his lack of skill at characterization. Greene and Malraux create complex, memorable characters whose personal moral struggles are anguished and poignant. In *Baraka*, Saul creates characters capable only of dealing with black-and-white conflicts between whether they should cheat and kill or decline to cheat and kill; they usually choose the former with much hesitation. Reviewers tended to treat the novel's ethics questions as simple and predictable, and they approached the novel more as a knowledgeable exposé of the oil business and the international arms trade than as a work of literature.

Perhaps this is what prompted Saul to devote much of his next novel, *The Next Best Thing,* to the moral self-analysis and self-justification of his characters. However, the basic materials of the novel are strikingly similar to those of the earlier ones. There is a solitary man on a quest: James Spenser, a young Briton who specializes in Burmese antiquities and who has recently resigned from the Victoria and Albert Museum; Spenser is infatuated with some eleventh-century Buddhas he hopes to steal from an abandoned Burmese temple. There is a conflict between bureaucracy and passion: Spenser has resigned from the Victoria and Albert because most of its staff "are paper scholars . . . more interested in careers than in beautiful objects" (29). He has left England because most of its citizens, especially the women, bore him with their passionless striving for material comfort and family respectability. He sees the Thai and Burmese jungles as places where he can be carried away from "the mediocrity of his former life, of London" and find "eternal freedom" (147). And while there are a number of semicomplex men in the novel—Spenser, the soldier-evangelist Blake, the ageing warlord Kung Minh, and the defeated and alcoholic British journalist Field—there is again only one significant woman. This time, her name is "Marea," and again she is, according to the narrator, consummately beautiful; once more, she joins the men in their homoerotic brotherhood by sleeping with each of them. Reinforcing the impression of a repeating pattern is the reappearance of several minor characters from *Baraka*.

Two of the reviewers of *The Next Best Thing* responded to Saul's literary claims by obediently mentioning Greene and by adding allusions to Joseph Conrad's jungle tale *The Heart of Darkness*. Don Cumming titled his *Maclean's* review "The Art of Darkness," and he went on to say that Saul's novel explores material "that was once the preserve of novelist Graham Greene." However, he added that the Saul version of Greene lacks "subtlety and economy." "There are echoes here of Conrad," wrote Tony Aspler in *Books in Canada*, explaining that Saul "has taken the political thriller out of its genre and given it the resonance and moral weight of the literary novel." A third reviewer, Barbara Black of the Montreal *Gazette*, noted the attempt at literariness:

"Saul has made an interesting effort to tackle the ethical questions posed by ancient-art-collecting, but he spoils it with exaggerated effects." A fourth, Thomas Schnurmacher, also of the *Gazette,* found that the moral concerns of the novel made it as "slow" as a jungle river, and that its various philosophical observations were pretentious, trite, and often "too lofty for a whoopee cushion."

Possibly, these reviewers were responding to the limited connections within the novel between ethical questioning and action. None of the characters' reflections deflect the course of the action or affect its outcome. Spenser, with the help of Blake and Field, plans an armed expedition through the chaotic border regions of Thailand and Burma to seize the statues; Khun Minh and others plot to double-cross or otherwise thwart them; Spenser, Blake, and their mostly South Asian party journey to the temple site, seize the statues, journey back, get into gun battles with Khun Minh's forces, suffer deaths and losses of statues, but eventually reach relative safety with four of the twenty Buddhas they have seized. As he did in *The Birds of Prey,* Saul uses arbitrary means to advance the plot—here inventing floods, ambushes, spooked pack animals, Blake's miraculous bush skills and marksmanship, and conveniently located secret trails—to keep the action moving homeward. On this framework of action the episodes of moral reflection hang like unnecessary decorations. In the final pages, Spenser ironically attains Buddhist nirvana—freedom from desiring either material or spiritual pleasure—when the remaining Buddhas that he manages to keep "swallow him into their purity." His sudden awareness of spirituality seems temporary and unconvincing, depending as it does on a melodramatic and hallucinatory moment of perception: "The six statues were crying out from their mules for pity and protection.

It was not a cry from the possessed to the possessor, but from beauty seeking to be one with him" (240). Spenser is, after all, the thief who is responsible for the statues' plight.

Saul does not have much skill at creating titles. His reasons for calling his first novel *The Birds of Prey* are unclear. There are no actual or metaphorical birds in the novel; its various right-wing plotters and assassins could be called jackals, snakes, or sharks as easily as birds. The narrator of Saul's second novel explains that *baraka* means "divine luck," but the plot contains no instances of such luck. *The Next Best Thing* is a similarly enigmatic title. It may refer to the fact that Spenser experiences art objects as more erotically stimulating than a beautiful woman—making the woman the next best thing. Maybe it has to do with Spenser's nirvana, and implies that this spiritual state, in which he can assure Marea that "it doesn't matter," is the next best thing to a humanistic, nonpragmatic life of meaningful action. Or perhaps the title is intended to indicate that successfully stealing six Buddha statues is the next best thing to stealing twenty. Perhaps Saul doesn't know.

The title of Saul's last novel, *The Paradise Eater* (1988), with its reference to Tennyson's lotus eaters, at least reflects the exploitative and self-indulgent lives its Western characters lead in Thailand. The novel's reviewers, however, were still distracted by Saul's self-comparisons to Naipaul and Greene. Tom Oleson began his *Winnipeg Free Press* review, "For a little while, at least for the first few pages of *The Paradise Eater,* you almost feel as if you are entering Graham Greene country . . . It's a good feeling, so when it turns out to be wrong, the disappointment is all the greater that in John Ralston Saul's latest novel we never get beyond the fringes of that world." In *Books in Canada,* Brian Fawcett wrote, "I wanted to read this book to figure out the fuss over John

Ralston Saul—why he's being compared to Graham Greene and Conrad. It turns out that Saul really is a contemporary master. The trouble is that it ain't writing he's good at. He's a master at market targeting." James Dunn in the *Vancouver Sun* concluded, "In terms of the writing, John Ralston Saul does not possess the psychological insight of someone like Graham Greene (whom he consciously seems to emulate)."

Nevertheless, while he was promoting *The Paradise Eater,* Saul persisted in making such comparisons. Reporting his conversation with Saul, Kenneth McGoogan of the *Calgary Herald* commented that the author had a penchant for making "literary pronouncements more sweeping than wise—dismissing Joyce, Roth, and Bellow in a single sentence, for example." McGoogan also remarked that Saul rejected "'self-indulgent, elitist' fiction" and wanted the novel to "reclaim its heritage as developed by Graham Greene and André Malraux." In a *Books in Canada* interview, Saul told Nancy Wigston, "I believe in lean writing, the Graham Greene-Malraux school . . . People like that were influenced by Conrad—he's the great dividing line in many ways." Wigston chided him for his masculinism: "Another male romantic?" Saul replied: "Absolutely. You describe very clearly what appears to be a physical adventure and what you're really doing is writing metaphysics."

The Paradise Eater was greeted with critical hostility, but it is the most substantial of the four novels. Although the mainspring of its action is a murder mystery, the central character, ex-journalist John Field, who played a relatively minor role in *The Next Best Thing,* is as absorbed by reflecting on his life as he is by solving the mystery. Field, now forty-four, had come to Bangkok from Montreal twenty years before. At the time, he was despairing over his failure to win his Westmount "dream girl"

(209). When the Vietnam War ended, he abandoned his journalism career and entered the more lucrative field of brokering shady business deals. Soon, Field was immersed in the underworld—a world of bribery, alcohol, venereal disease, and child prostitution. He fathered a daughter with one of his Thai mistresses, later sending the child to private school, and conscientiously concealed his "paradise eating" lifestyle from her.

When the novel opens, Field has a seemingly incurable strain of gonorrhoea. On an impulse, he's just purchased the contract of Ao, a beautiful seventeen-year-old venereal-disease-infected prostitute, and he's also about to leave for Vientiane in Laos to broker a trade for what is supposed to be heavy trucks and coffee; unknown to Field, the trade will likely include several tons of opium. A Canadian diplomat asks him to check on a Vientiane-based UN agricultural official, Charles Vadeboncoeur, and his wife, Diana—who is, in fact, Field's long-lost "dream girl." Field completes the business deal easily. Contacting the Vadeboncoeurs proves more difficult, and a day later he finds them brutally murdered and mutilated in their home. The Laotians attempt to frame him for the murder, but he escapes by swimming back to Thailand across the flood-swollen Mekong River. Once back in Bangkok, he is pursued by several determined assassins. They have evidently been dispatched by powerful people who believe that he possesses information, collected by Vadeboncoeur, on the Laotian government's opium business.

Perhaps it is Field's age and experience—all of Saul's other protagonists are callow youths by comparison—that give this novel more depth than the others. Field's ruminations on how Diana's refusal has affected him, on his responsibility to his daughter, and on his enjoyment of Ao's nonsexual companionship are presented concurrently with his frantic and unsuccessful attempts to discover who is trying to kill him. The novel ends with Field resolving his personal issues: he decides to return to Canada, giving up the easy but aimless life he has enjoyed thanks to the Western corruption of Thai culture; and he plans to take his daughter and Ao with him. Some reviewers—who evidently expected a conventional murder mystery—complained that this ending left the murders unsolved. In fact, they are solved as completely as they can be, given that they occur in secretive Laos, but Saul communicates the solution through a series of subtle clues, which he partly conceals beneath Field's increasing attention to his personal life.

This is not to say that *The Paradise Eater* is an especially strong novel. Field, who in *The Next Best Thing* was portrayed as alcoholic, cynical, defeated, and out of shape, is here portrayed as strong and athletic, despite the venereal infections that rack his body with fever. He outsprints assailants, wrestles a gun from a would-be assassin in a crowded bar, and effortlessly swims the Mekong. Ao is portrayed as the innocent prostitute who maintains her moral purity, kindness, intelligence, and good nature despite her six years in a brothel; it's implied that she'll make Field a sweet and supportive wife. Much of the narrative is composed of tediously repetitive taxi rides for which Field offers "thirty *baht*" to the driver. The taxi stalls in a flooded street, and Field arrives, pant cuffs dripping, in yet another prostitute-filled bar.

The foregrounded themes of the novel again arise from Saul's idée fixe of a pervasive Western conflict between pragmatism and humanism. Here, Diana is the symbol of pragmatism. She regards the working-class Field's affection and passion for her as inconvenient and diffidently lets him make love to her on three occasions, because to do so is less inconvenient than rejecting him outright. She then marries within her own class, thereby preserving her social status and wealth. Her pragmatism has so damaged Field, the novel argues, that he abandons his "dreams" and flees to Bangkok, where he can cynically and materialistically live "a boring little life" within a culture itself severely damaged by French and American imperialism (212). Field's reawakening from the lotus-eater life—through which he assumes responsibility for his daughter and altruistically rescues Ao— represents his return to the humanistic, nonpragmatic view of life that Diana wrenched him from.

Saul's "pleasure eater" allusion to Tennyson's "The Lotus Eaters" (itself based on a story of addiction from Homer's *Odyssey*) refers not only to the life of meaningless pleasure described in the poem but also to the nineteenth-century English practice of opium eating, to which the poem also indirectly alludes. Opium here is thus both the actual narcotic and a metaphor for Western imperialism. The North American demand for heroin corrupts South Asian society; the American and European demand for political and commercial dominance corrupts South Asian politics; the Western demand for easy sex and "sex-tourism" with almost-white Oriental girls corrupts South Asian family life.

Much as Saul's self-comparisons to Conrad, Greene, and Malraux say a great deal about his fantasy life as a writer, his novels say a great deal about his imaginative life in general. His imagination is populated by romantic, questing men and compliant, stereotypically beautiful, often Asian women. The men are loners or outsiders, attracted by adventure and beauty. The romance of the "true" attracts all of these men—the truth about General Ailleret's murder, the most truly beautiful wife, the most truly beautiful sculpture. Saul's women are much less concerned with the ideal, especially when it comes to sexual relations. For Melanie, Cosima, Marea, Diana, and Ao, sexual intercourse is interesting, but it's also physical and practical; for Spenser and Field, especially, it is magical and potentially life-defining. In interviews, Saul has attempted to differentiate among his male protagonists. To Wigston, for example, he suggested that Laing is "the modern ambitious man" and a "technocrat," Spenser is a man of obsession, and Field is an "escapee" from technocracy and "women's liberation and all those things." The latter remark implies that Saul sees women's liberation as part of the West's movement towards technocracy, pragmatism, and managerialism—that the pragmatic, modern, ambitious woman may be, like managerialism, something a man would be wise to flee.

Saul's imagination also tends to conjure scenes of raw power— in the offices of prime ministers and generals, and the exotic— those involving boar hunts at French chateaux, eleventh-century Burmese sculpture, the South Asian drug trade, and beautiful Oriental child prostitutes (an ironic fascination, given his relationship with Clarkson). Wigston challenged Saul on this fascination, and particularly on his sympathetic treatment of Field's relationships to Thai child prostitutes. She elicited three provocative responses. One was his assertion that out of every five hundred Thai girls in a brothel, "probably three hundred end up much better off than if they'd stayed in the rice paddies . . . So if you take the practical point of view, it sort of works as a system." Wigston did not appear to notice how odd it was of antipragmatist Saul to offer a "practical point of view." Saul's second response was that Westerners might be overly romantic about sex. "In the West there is an obsession that sex is essential to people growing up and to being sophisticated and a success . . . Sex has something to do with being perceived as being mature or immature, grown up or childish, a man or not a man, et cetera. In Bangkok sex is something you buy and sell; it's not very important." His third, and perhaps most provocative response was that very young girls may benefit from early sexual initiation because it could enable them to experience orgasm more easily later in life. He told Wigston that this theory, argued in the novel by his journalist character, Crappe, is based on an actual scientific study. He added that he hoped his novel would "force people to realize that what they believe to be absolute truths [he and Wigston had also discussed monogamy] are limited by both time and place."

Interestingly, Clarkson's two novels also suggest an imaginative life preoccupied with sexual adventure. Like Saul's, her books are populated with stereotypically exotic characters, and they reveal a similar preference for the exotic—which Clarkson finds in France rather than Bangkok. Her contrast between Canadian puritanism and the European understanding of sex as an aesthetic pleasure imprecisely parallels Saul's dichotomy between a pragmatic technocrat West and a South Asia that accepts sex with various partners as a daily pleasure. Regina Adler's openness to intercourse with any man who asks her "nicely," and the demythologizing of the sexual act that this implies, also parallel what Saul depicts as Thai sexual practice. By combining their six novels, one could conceive of some very curious multicultural viceregal soirees.

Adrienne Clarkson in a publicity shot for *Take 30*

Adrienne filming a segment for *Adrienne at Large*

Adrienne on location in Hong Kong for *Adrienne at Large*

Adrienne interviews Stephen Spender on *Take 30*

John Ralston Saul in a publicity shot for *The Paradise Eater*

Adrienne presents Pope John Paul II with a gift

Adrienne conducts an inspection of the guard at Rideau Hall

Mr. and Mrs. G.G. with some locals during a trip to Nunavut

With Britain's Queen Elizabeth at Balmoral Castle, Scotland

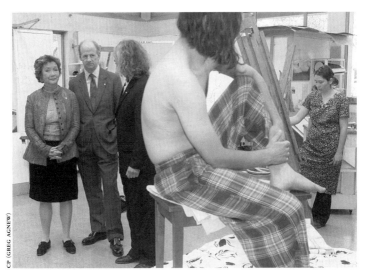

Observing a life drawing class at Mount Allison University

Adrienne holds up a copy of "Saul's Notes,"
prepared to help the media understand her husband's books

Adrienne greets the crowd on Canada Day

Viceregal Names

OR: John Ralston Clarkson
Philosopher Queen

Perhaps one should read the office of the governor general—with its carriages and footmen, its indoor tent, its white iron cross of the Order of Canada—as a work of genre fiction. Costumes, postures, and backdrops are all part of a politician's day. My puberty fantasies—including the ones about Princess Margaret—were a lot like Saul's novels. In one of them, me and my friends salvaged a scuttled U-boat and smuggled arms to liberation fighters in Africa. An ark for darkness. In the late 1940s, my dad's brother had a cute Chinese girlfriend. My mother was scandalized, but I was really impressed. My dad was impressed too.

Clarkson's novels aren't any more limited than Matt Cohen's first two novels or Marian Engel's first two novels. In my teen years, me and my friends had souped-up cars, which, like guns, also made good accessories. Maybe one could retell Princess Di's story as a version of *Clarissa*. Maybe Clarkson could have been a major novelist instead of a major performance artist. My car was a 1947 Ford coupe. People called me that kid, that hoodlum, that college student, that hot-rodder, that punk, that mixed-up kid. Hot-rods, of course, like French chateaux or fantasy U-boats, are conceptual art.

You don't need a shotgun. A very lethal .22 will do nicely. As long as it's pointed very, very well. (Clarkson, quoted by Diebel)

I'd have lunch with Hitler, if I thought it was part of my job. (Clarkson, quoted by Wong, 10 Sept. 1999)

Before the governor-general appointment, commentators had a relatively easy time finding categories for Adrienne Clarkson, but they had considerable difficulty finding a category for John Ralston Saul. For Clarkson, they usually resorted to the relatively neutral terms that described her employment: "broadcaster," "agent general," "diplomat," "publisher," or "host and executive producer of CBC Television's *Adrienne Clarkson Presents.*" Sometimes, they would string a series of factual categories together to indicate her versatility: "television personality and author" (Flohil), "author and well-known Canadian TV personality" ("Publishers"). Some commentators would add terms that indicated their disapproval of the way Clarkson cheerfully embraced wealth and elite international culture.

In 1985, John Fraser of the *Globe and Mail* affectionately called her "La Clarkson." Then he mentioned not only her "panache" and "smartly decorated" Paris office but also the fact that a CBC researcher once referred to her as a "pushy bitch." "Clarkson is a name-dropper," Antonia Zerbesias began her *Toronto Star* column in 1989; "she has her own imprint at M&S, her 'designer label.'" CBC's Air Farce comedy team repeatedly parodied Clarkson's television byline, "I'm Adrienne Clarkson," with the line "I'm Adrienne Clarkson, and you're not!"—possibly alluding to the way in which Clarkson associated herself with high culture such as opera, ballet, poetry, and prize-winning fiction, and "not" with mass-cultural forms such as soap opera, situation comedy, and pop music. Most commentators, however, presented her association with high culture relatively favourably. For example, Andrew Cohen, discussing Clarkson's representation of Ontario in France, remarked, "Cosmopolitan, bilingual, and elegant, she was a natural for Paris"—although "for Paris" puts an edge on the description and implies that she may not be "a natural" for Canada. Later in his mostly factual article, Cohen called Clarkson "cocky and animated."

Terms like "Chinese," "Chinese-Canadian," "immigrant," and "refugee" were occasionally attached to Clarkson before her appointment as governor general, but only in descriptions of her remote background. Catherine Breslin's 1969 sketch "Adrienne Clarkson: TV's Cool Lady" is representative of this view of Clarkson that foregrounded her broadcasting career and marvelled somewhat sardonically at her other accomplishments: "a genuine intellectual," "the compleat wife," "a little amazon of organization." Although she had a seemingly unconscious tendency to call Clarkson "inscrutable," Breslin mentioned her subject's Asianness mostly to make the point that it's anomalous—strange or surprising, because it is so easily forgotten.

McCracken's 1972 *Maclean's* profile normalized Clarkson's Asianness by evoking it in highly positive terms—"the beautiful Hong Kong-born woman," "the dark, serious, brilliant, romantic, Chinese woman she is, a lady," "her style and her voice are upperclass Anglo Saxon; they contradict her Oriental features"—and by burying these references within hundreds more to New York fashion, French culture, and Toronto politics. However, the subliminal indicator of Chineseness, "inscrutable," appeared again. Clarkson's photo was featured on the magazine's cover with a caption that read, "Adrienne Clarkson: Scrutinizing the Inscrutable," presumably composed by a *Maclean's* editor.

Except for Breslin's ironic "genuine intellectual" (indicating, perhaps, that some may have mistaken her for a pseudointellectual?), almost none of the terms that writers used to describe Clarkson suggested that she was a person of ideas. She was a conveyor of other people's ideas, a broadcaster, a diplomat, a publisher. Breslin even wondered why Clarkson had a reputation in Canadian media circles for exceptional intelligence: "Maybe it's the fact that so few other Canadian TV stars write novels in Uzbekistan that makes people see Adrienne as a little shinier than life. She's got a good enough head on her narrow shoulders, but why do people describe her as 'a fabulous intelligence,' 'an enormous intellect,' 'a really tremendous brain'?" Unfortunately, Breslin didn't attribute these appraisals, so the reader couldn't determine how much credence they deserved or what may have motivated them.

"Immigrant" and "refugee" started to be emphasized as terms for Clarkson only after she became governor general. Such categories, and the qualifications they imply, were apparently irrelevant to her role as host for CBC Television's *Take 30* or *The Fifth Estate*, or to her roles as Ontario's agent general in France and publisher of McClelland and Stewart. These terms were, however, quickly activated by the Liberal government in making the viceregal appointment. In his announcement, Prime Minister Jean Chrétien described the appointment as "a reflection of the diversity and inclusiveness of our society and an indication of how much our country has matured over the years." In accepting, Clarkson began by saying, "I am honoured to be the first woman of neither founding nation to be governor general of Canada . . . I am the first immigrant, I am originally a refugee . . ." (Ditchburn).

In the years that followed, Clarkson employed Chrétien's words, "diversity" and "inclusiveness," and her own word, "immigrant," in approximately fifty percent of her viceregal speeches. By invoking such categories in his announcement, the prime minister had, in a sense, recast Clarkson's identity; he had also specified the attributes that, in his view, had qualified her for the position. She had been appointed governor general in order to highlight Canada's multiculturalism and social maturity. The appointment had not necessarily been made to demonstrate the nation's high-culture accomplishments, or to grace the office of the governor general with intelligence, beauty, style, or elegance. Journalist Juliet O'Neill noticed Clarkson's newly remodelled identity: "Clarkson cast herself at a news conference Wednesday as the first immigrant-refugee governor-general. Both she and Chrétien suggested the appointment is intended to symbolize Canada's ethnic diversity" ("Broadcaster").

The newspaper headlines that followed her appointment tended to present four Clarksons: the familiar television personality (O'Neill, "Broadcaster"); the successful refugee and immigrant (Steed); the smug, self-important elitist, occasionally glimpsed before (Steyn, "Long Live Queen Adrienne"); and the dangerous left-wing activist, rarely seen before (Fife, "Activists"). Some newspapers attempted to present several identities. In the Montreal *Gazette*, Joan Bryden wrote: "Veteran broadcaster and arts doyen Adrienne Clarkson has become the first member of a visible minority to be named governor-general of Canada." A *Gazette* editorial, written by Norman Webster, offered narrower but even more conflicting identities: "Adrienne Clarkson is feisty, flinty, glamorous, brainy, ravenously ambitious, and ferociously energetic."

The general shift here is from professional categories such as broadcaster or author to official and public categories such as immigrant, refugee, and activist. According to the rhetoric of these comments, it was not remarkable that the prime minister had appointed a broadcaster or an author or even an intellectual to the office, but it was remarkable that he'd appointed an immigrant or a refugee, and it was regrettable that he may have appointed an activist or someone "ravenously ambitious." As a result, Clarkson's public identity expanded and shifted slightly. She was perceived as "more Chinese" than she'd been previously, and she was now more refugee than broadcaster, more immigrant than author. "The fact that I'm Chinese doesn't mean anything to me," she had told Breslin in 1969. "My husband says I'm more Anglo-Saxon than he is." In her installation speech, however, Clarkson identified herself and her parents not only as refugees and immigrants but also as Chinese who, between 1926 and 1949, could not "arrive as part of a regular immigration procedure. There was no such thing for a Chinese family at that time in Canadian history." Those commentators interested in the backgrounds of Chinese Canadians especially and understandably focused on Clarkson's racial heritage. One was Frank Ching, who published the article "Canada Honours a Chinese" in the *Far Eastern Economic Review.* The Internet bulletin boards of worldwide Taishan-origin immigrants and of Hakka-origin people on the Asian Wind Web site were briefly flooded with pleased and marvelling comments.

But a peculiar undercurrent to Clarkson's appointment and installation and the strong new invocations of her Chineseness was provided by the arrival on Canada's West Coast of several ships loaded with illegal Chinese migrants, most of whom were en route to New York City. Many Canadian newspapers, including the *Globe and Mail,* juxtaposed their September 9 front-page announcements of her appointment with a similarly large instalment of the continuing story of the migrants, variously titled "Navy Tracking Suspect Ship" (*Globe and Mail*), "Navy on Alert" (*Calgary Herald*), "Navy Tracks Fifth Suspect Ship" (*Vancouver Sun*). The juxtapositions seemed inadvertent, since the story of the Chinese migrants and those dangerously derelict ships had been front-page news for most of the summer. However, they did lead one newspaper cartoonist to note the implicit irony and to create a cartoon that, according to James Brooke of the *New York Times,* "secretly pleased" Clarkson. "In the cartoon, a Mountie sternly looked down at a huddled boatload of illegal Chinese immigrants, then warned a fellow Mountie to be careful because 'one of them could be a future Governor General.'" And Rosemary Sexton in the *National Post* observed, "this extraordinarily accomplished former Hong Kong refugee is taking on one of the highest offices of the land, albeit a ceremonial one, at the same time as hordes of Chinese refugees try to enter this country illegally" ("Sense"). Sexton's "hordes," incidentally, were at that point fewer than six hundred people.

Jan Wong, taking advantage of her own Chinese credentials, joined in with a number of remarks. These included, "I'm . . .

very glad that she's an ethnic Chinese, considering the resurgence of Yellow Perilism as Boat Four looms off the B.C. coast"; and, "She just doesn't seem, well, like a Chinese refugee" ("Says 'She's Adrienne Clarkson'"). Wong was, in effect, reversing Sexton's paradox of glamorous Adrienne versus threatening Chinese "hordes" to create one of hysterical Canadian racism versus ethnicity-shirking Adrienne. A month later, Wong expanded these remarks, making fun of the Chinese elements Clarkson had included in the new viceregal coat of arms. She accused Clarkson of "playing the Chinese card a bit too late" and pointed out that Clarkson had "kept her first husband's non-Chinese surname, even as she airbrushed *him* from her *Who's Who* entry 20 years ago." Despite the seeming justness of this particular criticism, Wong's article was vicious in tone, and it suggested some personal feelings beyond those visible in the points she raised. Wong sarcastically mentioned Clarkson's estrangement from her two now-adult daughters and coyly implied that Clarkson had betrayed her Chineseness, and that of her daughters, in order to pursue her individual ambitions. Clarkson was now only accepting a Chinese identity, Wong maintained, because Chrétien had "set her up": "All this Chinese-roots stuff is probably not her fault. Prime Minister Jean Chrétien has set her up, announcing that she would be the 'first visible minority' governor-general and 'the first Canadian [one] not born in Canada.' What are you supposed to do after that? Pretend you come from Yorkville?" ("On Madame Clarkson").

Confronted over her columns by students at the University of British Columbia's Sing Tao School of Journalism, Wong protested, "Do you think it's wrong of me to say she's not part of the Chinese community, she never did anything for the Chinese community and that she never identified with it? I think that's relevant. I don't say it's bad, I'm just pointing it out." But the rhetoric and tone of Wong's columns had characterized Clarkson's non-Chineseness as much worse than "bad." The journalism student reporting Wong's protest juxtaposed the story with an opinion of journalists voiced by ex-premier of B.C. Mike Harcourt: "poor ethical training in journalism schools makes journalists think they are a law unto themselves." This piece, set in bold face, continued: "The arrogance of the press, says Harcourt, is wrapped in the belief that they inhabit a higher moral plane than the democratically elected representatives of the people and that they know how to run the government better than those appointed to do the job" (Sagar).

A few journalists hinted that Clarkson had received the appointment undeservedly because of her race and gender. Hugh Winsor of the *Globe and Mail* wrote that she was chosen because "it was time for a woman," and because she provided the additional "bonus" of "her Chinese ancestry." In the *Toronto Sun*, Allan Fotheringham concealed his objections beneath his claim of being Clarkson's "buddy": "It's been an open secret in media and political circles that my old buddy, not a woman to trifle with, has been lobbying heavily in Ottawa for either the CBC presidency or Rideau Hall. Visible minority, political correctness, all that." From this view, it was only a small step to the cynicism and sarcasm of the *Toronto Sun's* Connie Woodcock: "At this rate, the next governor-general will have to be gay and handicapped—an opportunity, perhaps, for Svend Robinson, should he break a leg or require glasses. Gay, handicapped and Inuit would be nice."

Writing in the academic journal *Canadian Literature*, Glenn Deer found these linkages, various media comments (although he seemed unaware of those of Wong, Fotheringham, and

Woodcock), and Clarkson's new casting as "Chinese" extremely troubling. He suggested—unknowingly agreeing with Wong, but without endorsing her ideology—that Chinese was not an identity Clarkson had chosen. He argued, like Wong, that it had been forced upon her by the specific rhetoric of the prime minister. "The Asian label is not one that Clarkson went seeking," Deer wrote, "it was applied to her in order to promote the image of Canadian social inclusiveness." He wondered if the term "refugee" would have been invoked if she'd arrived in 1942 "from London or Dublin" rather than Hong Kong. He argued that the new labels people were applying to her both praised and diminished her—they professed "the mobility of the individual while limiting it by implying she is somehow less Canadian because of her refugee past." This language holds Clarkson up "as the model refugee migrant, the fully assimilated Canadian" and "subtly embeds her in the category of the Other, the 'new' Canadian."

Also like Wong, Deer identified himself in his article as a Chinese Canadian. His main focus here was on Asian Canadian writing and on the principle that he believed much of this literature upholds: individuals should have control over their cultural identifications. Towards the end of the piece, Deer cited the Chinese American David Henry Hwang: "More important than race, national origin, or genetic heritage are those groups and individuals that define *themselves* in response to shared experiences, frustrations, and needs. The factor of self-definition becomes the key . . . immigrants become Americans when and if they choose to define themselves as such." He concluded by wishing for himself, and others of Asian background, "this kind of mobility . . . beyond the constraints of racial category."

The issues Deer raises are perhaps much more complex than

he indicates, and so is the relationship between individual self-assertion and social interaction and definition. An individual is always in a social context and is perceived and self-perceived differently as that context changes. In general, "Chineseness" has become more permissible and more important to many Chinese Canadians as Canada has become more multicultural. Although the word "Chinese" had not frequently been attached to Clarkson before, and although she had denied its importance in her 1969 interview with Breslin, she had publicly identified herself as Chinese several times, most notably when she journeyed to China in 1979. She visited her ancestral village and later published a thirteen-page account of her trip, "Understanding Hearts," in the mass-circulation *Weekend Magazine*. In 1980, she again publicized her Chineseness in an article called "Beginnings," which dealt with her immigration and childhood; and in 1981, she published the article "Poor No More," about early Chinese immigrants to Canada whom she called her "relatives." Both pieces appeared in the mass-circulation *Today* magazine. In 1983, while serving as Ontario's agent general in Paris, she quipped to a Toronto audience that the French "are among the most intelligent in the world—except for the Chinese" (Aumon). This flash of humour suggests that, at the very least, she was comfortable about being perceived as Chinese. When protesting NAFTA in 1988, she prefaced her remarks with, "As an immigrant."

Wong may have been too young to notice such things and too rushed to look for them. At the news conference for the announcement of her appointment, Clarkson did not seem shocked by Chrétien's characterization of her as a personification of Canadian diversity. On the contrary, she appeared to welcome it as a reflection of her own self-assertion as an "immigrant" and a "refugee."

And yet Wong and Deer may be right that Clarkson's options at the news conference were limited, that the appointment required her to accept a "new" or "multicultural" or "Chinese" Canadian identity. Chrétien's framing of the announcement was also—as Wong and Deer failed to mention—politically self-serving, since it further entrenched the Liberal Party as the party of immigration, immigrants, tolerance, and multiculturalism. Moreover, Clarkson appeared to move slightly towards Deer's position in her installation speech to Parliament. She expressed her gratitude to her grade school teachers for having treated her as "bright" rather than "bright yellow." Perhaps the prime minister had indeed come uncomfortably close to welcoming her as "bright yellow."

The increased frequency and vehemence with which the "I'm Adrienne Clarkson, and you're not" characterization of Clarkson—snobbish, excessively ambitious, overly impressed with her own accomplishments—was deployed after her appointment was probably due to two causes. One was that the governor generalship is a patronage appointment, and it highlights the appointee's connections to the federal ruling party much more than it does his or her relative merits. Calgary West MP Rob Anders clearly linked the patronage and the cultural superiority issues when he called the appointment "a patronage leap-frog" and protested, "She's a well-known elitist" (Bryden, "Clarkson a Governor General"). Anders also remarked that the posting "should have been reviewed by a parliamentary committee before being made." Indeed, the job is never nationally advertised—as are, for example, university professorships and presidencies—to ensure fairness and integrity in the hiring process. A prime minister cannot claim to have considered all plausible candidates.

A second cause for the new emphasis on Clarkson's perceived

elitism is the way in which the appointment implicitly included Clarkson's partner, John Ralston Saul, as at least a junior part of the governor generalship. Saul was already widely considered in the media to be a dubious quantity, to be arrogant, pompous, condescending, and quite possibly a cultural and intellectual pretender. A few months before Clarkson's appointment, an *Ottawa Citizen* editorial described him as "intellectual poseur John Ralston Saul" and condemned his recommendation to University of Western Ontario graduates that they take their time in finding a job ("Go Ahead"). Immediately after the appointment, the *Citizen*'s David Warren wrote a column entitled "Intellectual Fraud Parades as Genius," in which he suggested that Saul reads only the dust jackets of the books he cites.

Even during Saul's years at Petro-Canada, some had viewed him as a bit of a prima donna. Douglas Bowie, a former Petro-Canada vice president, recalled that Saul would order "'a sherry with two lumps of ice' and it would come back and there would be three ice cubes and he'd send it back" (Lownsbrough). In 1979, Olivia Ward, setting out to interview the young novelist who had just published *The Birds of Prey*, encountered various extreme views of the man: "'Why should I meet John Ralston Saul,' a successful 40-year-old writer asked me. 'If I got to know him it would ruin the miserable pleasure of wanting to be the son-of-a-bitch.' A little extreme, perhaps. But typical of those who've followed the career of the best-selling author of *Birds of Prey*—a man heralded as a new André Malraux . . . For the Ralston Saul portfolio includes such international credits as scholar, entrepreneur, journalist, and political adviser on two continents, before you get around to the novel. Worse, he's a man who, at the age of 31, has also acquired a reputation for style, wit, and a certain cachet. ('Whatever you call it,' grumbles columnist Allan Fotheringham, 'it's attracted Canada's most fascinating woman.') And a Cabbagetown neighbour of Ralston Saul and broadcaster Adrienne Clarkson adds, 'they're Sartre and de Beauvoir—with looks.'" And in 1995, Val Ross reported that Saul "is known to refuse Perrier at dinner parties and to request more arcane mineral waters."

Early in his career, Saul was usually identified as a novelist with a strange background: several years as a vice president of Petro-Canada. Once he began publishing books on the history and limitations of twentieth-century managerial culture, precisely who or what he was became more uncertain. Lownsbrough expressed this uncertainty when he began his article on Saul, "In the tight little confluence of circles making up the world of CanLit, Saul is a bit of an anomaly . . . in part because of the role he has contrived for himself as author and social activist." Here, Lownsbrough's reservations and hesitations are directed specifically at whether Saul is literary: As an author of adventure novels and the cultural history *Voltaire's Bastards*, does he really belong in "CanLit"? Lownsbrough also wonders whether Saul is genuine: Is his cultural role self-contrived?

The reviews of Saul's nonfiction titles—*Voltaire's Bastards: The Dictatorship of Reason in the West* (1992), *The Doubter's Companion: A Dictionary of Aggressive Common Sense* (1994), *The Unconscious Civilization* (1995), *Reflections of a Siamese Twin: Canada at the End of the Twentieth Century* (1997), and *On Equilibrium* (2001)—mirror this uncertainty. Leslie Armour, reviewing *Voltaire's Bastards* for the *Canadian Forum,* identified Saul as "a Toronto historian, thriller writer, and one-time oil executive." Stan Persky in the *Globe and Mail* dubbed Saul a "lone polymath" and "gentleman amateur." Michael Harrison, reviewing the book for the *Financial Post,* called him a "novelist" and an "intellectual Odysseus." In his *Quill and Quire* review of *The Doubter's Companion,* John Lorinc identified Saul as "a celebrity controversialist." John Geddes, reviewing *The Unconscious Civilization* for the *Financial Post,* described Saul as "shaping up as a full-blown pop phenomenon" and asked, "What's he on about?" Jamie Swift, *Queen's Quarterly* reviewer for *Reflections of a Siamese Twin,* called Saul "a popularizer of ideas" rather than an original thinker; Christopher Moore, reviewing the same book for *The Beaver,* labelled him "a novelist and essayist"; Nelson Wiseman in *Quill and Quire* declared him "a popularizing philosopher"; and Peter C. Newman of *Maclean's* called him "part polemicist, part philosopher." Reviewing *On Equilibrium,* an *Ottawa Citizen* writer described Saul as a "defiant thinker" ("The Man"). Also writing about *On Equilibrium, Vancouver Sun* columnist George Fetherling called him "a patrician of humble origins."

Like Newman, most of these reviewers hedged their bets as to what Saul could be by yoking contrasting terms. A "celebrity controversialist" may be more interested in celebrity than in ideas; a "popularizer of ideas" or a "popularizing philosopher" may be more interested in popularity than in philosophic integrity.

The reviews also reveal that when Saul's *On Equilibrium* appeared, a little more than a year after Clarkson's appointment, the commentary took on a slightly more contentious tone. Mark Bourrie, reviewing for the *Hill Times,* called Saul "the philosopher John Ralston Saul," but he titled his review "John Ralston Saul Sets Table for Lively Appetizing Political Talk"—a mischievous reference to Clarkson-Saul dinner table conversations predicted by Jean Chrétien. Rebecca Wigod, in the *Vancouver Sun,* identified the book as part three of Saul's "philosophical trilogy." However, a *Calgary Sun* editorial on the book, entitled "Saul's

Timing Bad, But His Argument Is Even Worse," described Saul as "a self-styled public philosopher" who was "trained in philosophy" (he wasn't); the *Edmonton Journal* called him a "professional starter of controversies" ("Saul Respects Limits"); the *National Post*'s Mark Steyn referred to the author sarcastically as "one of the intellectual colossi of the age" ("The Prince Consort"); Hubert Beyer in the *Kimberley Daily Bulletin* described him nonsarcastically as "one of Canada's great minds"; Claire Hoy in the *Sudbury Star* charged that he was "an arrogant, self-serving blowhard" posing "as a great intellectual"; Jack Knox, in the *Victoria Times-Colonist,* called him "an ill-humoured, elitist Rex Murphy"; Charles Gordon, reproaching Saul in the *Ottawa Citizen* for having used the title "Excellency" to promote his book, suggested that he adopt "Excellency" as his pen name but added (turning Saul's various prodemocracy arguments against him) that "there is no reason why anyone should call him or herself 'excellency' in a democratic society"; in the *Victoria Times-Colonist*, Lawrence Martin wrote that Saul was "the world's only man, to quote a dry wit, who can strut while sitting down." Echoed here were the April 2000 remarks of Stephen Harper, then head of the right-wing National Citizens' Coalition: Saul, he said, "is a friend of the government's philosophy of the country... a binational, multi-ethnic state ... not a serious scholar," adding, "Saul is such an intellectual lightweight that a 10 km wind would blow him right off the ground" (Bunner). Amid the cacophony of these characterizations, the *Ottawa Citizen*'s Alison Korn offered the difficult-to-understand description of Saul as "respected author."

Most of the negative characterizations of Saul have focused on his credentials. They point out that he is self-constructed or self-styled as an expert rather than authorized as such by others. Professional historians and philosophers note that he does not invite dialogue with scholars of history or philosophy—that he often does not cite his sources so that others can check and interpret them, that his work is not peer reviewed, that his books are not published by academic publishing houses, which generally check facts and references. They also observe that Saul does not engage in discussions with the leading historians and philosophers of his time, and that he does not, therefore, place his work in the context of the disciplines he claims to practice. Those who have honoured him with the title "philosopher" have been, for the most part, journalists untrained in philosophy who employ the term in its popular sense of "knowledgeable person" or "deep thinker." Or they assume that philosophers are people who present themselves as being wise, or who purport to have useful insights or "answers." Is Saul a philosopher? Not in the strict sense of one who is principally engaged by questions of epistemology, the study of the difficulties and uncertainties of knowing anything. He is not a philosopher if we understand that designation to mean someone who appreciates the fragility of all argument, who knows that all statements are hypothetical and will inevitably be qualified or rendered problematical by future thinkers.

Interestingly, the credentials argument advanced by the various journalists who have criticized Saul is not all that different from the argument of professional scholars. They too insist that Saul is "self-styled," that he has no advanced degree in philosophy, that he has not remained within the discipline of history, in which he earned his doctorate, and is therefore not a proper historian. They have also suggested that by seeking the approval of a nonacademic readership, Saul is merely trying to impress the unknowledgeable, and that he may be nervous about discussing his ideas with people who have actually read the books he claims to have read.

Clarkson married Saul on July 31, 1999, ostensibly to smooth the way for her acceptance of the governor generalship. That, coupled with the government's implied promise that Saul would have a viceregal role, caused Adrienne Clarkson's public image, for the first time, to be shaded by the uncertainties and suspicions attached to her longtime partner. Exactly why the government, and particularly the prime minister, allowed the appointment to be perceived as a package deal, incorporating Saul's lengthy biography into the official press release, is obscure—although it was amusingly consistent with media characterizations of Saul as a figure with an inflated estimation of himself. Though the government did not require Saul to take an oath of office, it allowed him to act as if he was, at the very least, a deputy governor general. He could post his speeches on the official Rideau Hall Web site and give viceregal addresses even when the governor general was not ill or otherwise engaged (filling in during illness had been a practice for many earlier viceregal spouses).

Chrétien's clumsy observation that, with his historical and philosophical knowledge, Saul might be able to help Clarkson— "Her husband is a very well-known writer and wrote about politics and sociology and what not. So I guess that over dinner they might, between the two of them, come [up] with a pretty good conclusion"—was correctly read by Maude Barlow as masculinist and patronizing. "If she didn't understand something political," speculated Barlow, "she could have a chat with her husband at dinner" (Cheadle). Barlow's interpretation, in fact, seems generous. Chrétien's various qualifiers and restrictions—"might . . . come up, " "pretty good," and "between the two of them"— strongly implied that Clarkson would be unlikely to come up with a "good conclusion" about things political or sociological on her own.

The effect of the package presentation was that the public began to perceive of Clarkson and Saul as a unit. Their differences, apparently, were minimal. "Articulate, outspoken, bilingual, educated and left-leaning, Clarkson and Saul are among the cream of the Canadian literati and arts set," wrote Bruce Cheadle. "Adrienne Clarkson and writer John Ralston Saul have used their celebrity to wade into a variety of political debates," declared Luiza Chwialkowska in the *National Post,* in an article called "Couple Used to Taking Political Centre Stage." "The Clarkson-Saul tandem will bring a certain zest to the office," predicted Jeffrey Simpson in a column titled "The Two-Headed Governor-General." On the far right, Canada First director Paul Fromm chimed in with an openly racist and satirically "royal" commentary entitled "The Dragon Queen and His Banality." "The famously brainy duo—media darling and philosopher king—promise to put a new kind of shine on the G-G's crown," commented Paula Brook, with equal hostility, in the *Vancouver Sun.* "What we're looking at here are double-barrelled ideologues with a big budget, big agenda, and big platform. It's double your pleasure if you happen to agree with them." Brook then noted that Saul and Clarkson had given substantially the same speech to two different B.C. audiences and wondered whose mouth was speaking through whose: "It's just a bit unnerving . . . to see her open her mouth and him talk. And vice versa."

This confusion of Clarkson and Saul as G.G. and "G.G.2" not only obscured certain differences between them, but it also caused words such as "left-leaning" to be applied to Clarkson for the first time (Bunner). This is not to deny that Clarkson had been articulate on the liberal or the liberal left sides of various issues. But, unlike Saul, she had not attempted to construct a general historical and economic view within which to interpret particular issues. Saul's critiques of reason, managerialism, pragmatism, and "Harvard MBAs" were openly political and ideological and offered a template for the interpretation of certain issues—the arms trade, sex tourism, drug smuggling, educational goals. Clarkson's public positions on abortion, the arts, and free trade could be read as modestly informed sympathies or enthusiasms rather than elements of a politically informed, ideologically consistent analysis.

In the years since the appointment, public concern over the irregularity of a two-headed governor general has waned—except on two fronts. People are still troubled about the sales advantage the position may be giving Saul as an author and about the propriety of a quasi-official governor general, such as Saul, making statements that are contrary to the diplomatic or economic interests of the nation. When *On Equilibrium*—with its unflattering portrayal of President George Bush and its suggestion that Christian civilization had earned the Islamic enmity that motivated the Al Qaeda attack on the World Trade Center—came out in the fall of 2001, it prompted *Edmonton Sun* editorialist Neil Waugh to declare the viceregal pair "elite and aloof left-wing snobs who have failed to check their politics at the door when they took up residence at Rideau Hall." Waugh then expanded his attack to include the Canadian arts. When he reviled "state-supported culture," the reference to Clarkson's old employer, the CBC—and the writers, opera singers, and ballet dancers her shows had celebrated—was clear. "This kind of anti-American claptrap," Waugh continued, "is rampant in the elite ranks of Canada's state-supported culture. It's an obscure little club that a vast majority of ordinary Canadians have never heard of. And, if they're lucky, never will."

A *Charlottetown Guardian* December 15, 2001 editorial suggested that Clarkson might decide "it was time for hubby to put his philosophy career on hold" and correctly observed that one of the difficulties with the package arrangement was that while Saul was free to act as if he were the governor general, he "didn't take the same oaths as Clarkson did and technically is free to say whatever he wants." The *Guardian* had identified the anomaly of Saul's position: that he was enjoying most of the advantages, perks, and authority of the governor generalship without being subject to its rules.

An opinion column in the *Sudbury Star* came very close to offering the same analysis, blaming the situation partly on the prime minister for having implied "that Clarkson and Saul would operate as a team in her new role." It also blamed Clarkson herself for having suggested that "Canadians have a couple who act as partners in the Governor-General's office." The column then maintained that such statements should be ignored, and that "when Saul acts like he's important because of the airs of the Governor-General's office he should be ignored." The piece concluded with the democratic assertion that "John Ralston Saul doesn't deserve the respect or attention of anyone just because he happens to be married to Canada's Governor-General" ("Saul's View"). Like several of the other objectors, the writer of this column was speaking from an angry populist position, as the assertion of "airs" and refusal of "respect" indicate. But, legally and constitutionally, because Saul did not take a joint oath to undertake the duties and responsibilities of the office, it is difficult to defend the way he's used his public and governor general's

Web site speeches to give the impression that he speaks and writes in the voice of that office. One of Saul's literary models, author Graham Greene, makes the point in his novel *The Heart of the Matter* that a corrupt and drunken "whiskey priest" performs the ceremonies of the Church, such as confession, baptism, or mass, purely and authentically despite his corruption. This is because he does so as a stand-in—through his vows and ordination—for Christ, and at those moments he is not a fallible human. Clarkson, similarly, as I noted earlier, stands in through her oath of office—like the queen herself—for the authority of the Crown. In her official capacity, she enacts the office, not her own person or its failings. This is not Saul's situation, legally, ethically, or constitutionally.

Yet we may indeed have what is functionally a two-headed—or perhaps a one-and-a-half-headed—governor general. As I explore in detail in the next chapter, Clarkson has taken many of the central ideas of her speeches—that Canada is constitutionally one of the oldest countries in the world; that Canada is a northern and therefore socialist nation; that Canada has a long history of creative political compromise; that Canada was established on a "triangular foundation" of aboriginal, anglophone, and francophone peoples; that public education has been essential to Canada's reception of immigrants; that public service and responsible citizenship are threatened by contemporary commercial culture—almost verbatim from Saul's writings. She usually does this without acknowledgement. In this unique viceregal package arrangement, there are often two mouths to utter the speeches but only one set of ideas.

After Clarkson's installation, more controversy arose about her name and Saul's. What was one to call Mr. Saul? "Canada's First Husband," Paul Bunner proposed in *The Report,* "deputy governor-general," suggested Colin Grey in the *Ottawa Citizen*, "philosopher king," ventured John Geddes in *Maclean's*. Laura Penny in *Toronto Life* drew a brief comparison between Saul and Pope John Paul II. Each had three names, she observed, and both were "balding do-gooders" who had succeeded by marrying well—the pope to the Church and Saul to Clarkson. Rideau Hall announced that Saul would be called "Your Excellency," to the dismay of acting opposition leader John Reynolds. Clarkson retorted that the title was traditional: "It's not done in a grovelling and strange manner, it's only a way of address. It's part of etiquette" (O'Neill, "Clarkson").

A similar controversy had arisen when Rideau Hall announced that the governor general preferred to be addressed as "Madame Clarkson." "Adrienne Clarkson Is 'Madame,' And You're Not," the *National Post* headlined a story by Richard Foot. In it, Foot pondered whether "Madame" might be a French word rather than an English one. Alliance MP Deborah Grey cracked jokes about what "madams" were in the Canadian West and added a jab at Saul's three-barrelled name: "I wonder how she asks him to bring a quart of milk home? 'John Ralston Saul, please bring me some two percent?'" (Naumetz). However, dictionaries indicate that both *madam* and *madame* exist in English, with *madam* designating a woman of rank or office, as in "madam president," and *madame* being a "title of distinction." If Clarkson and Saul hadn't brought to Rideau Hall solid reputations as elitist and (in his case) pretentious elitist, it's unlikely that her desire to be addressed as "Madame" or his to be addressed as "Excellency" would have raised an eyebrow; such requests hadn't raised eyebrows in the case of previous governors general and their spouses. But in light of the Clarkson-Sauls' earlier assertions of class and taste, both titles seemed to be for their new bearers dreams come true.

Viceregal Ideas

OR: O Lead Heavenly Light
Helping Lesser People

That was a second pass through my pile of clippings. What's in a name?—grievance, ambition, envy, vanity, fear, anger, and a lot more fantasies. One of my great-grandmothers was a United Empire Loyalist from Pennsylvania. I don't think that has much to do with me, but it might. Life's not a cabaret, it's a costume party, and only sometimes do people get to pick their own costumes. (Not nearly often enough, says Glenn Deer.) The way I see it, J.R. Saul is entitled to think the best of himself, and I'm entitled to be sceptical and cheeky. One of my great-great-grandmothers was Métis, but in India many people regard me as part of the great British diaspora. Life's not a cabaret, it's a theatre set, and sometimes we have to perform tragedy or farce or romantic comedy just to keep our hopes in sight, or our jobs. The problem with self-construction is that we live in a society of competing constructors. Another problem with self-construction is that sometimes the foundation doesn't pass inspection. One of my grandmothers was named Kirkup—she descended from guys who sailed Viking ships to England. She was part of the great Norse diaspora. The problem with trying to construct others is that most often our efforts only construct ourselves. Life for Mr. and Mrs. G.G. is not a cabaret, it's press clippings and rubber chickens and having to give cheerful speeches even when you have nothing to talk about except four or five ideas one of you had twenty years ago.

"Imaginative creation" can be offered as an image of non-alienated labour; the intuitive, transcendental scope of the poetic mind can provide a living criticism of those rationalist or empiricist ideologies enslaved to "fact." (Eagleton 19)

From the beginning, in her role as television host for cultural or public affairs programs, Clarkson has encountered ideas at the ground level. At this level, ideas come in the form of particular events or particular people rather than pieces of larger patterns. Television, as Marshall McLuhan noted, is especially good at the close-up. It offers a fragmentary but intimate view of the world— a particular plane crash, a new folksinger, a new problem with gasoline prices or French fries. Clarkson's early CBC work was mostly on two contrasting public affairs shows: the soft-focus afternoon information show *Take 30*, and the more abrasive investigative show (modelled on CBS's *60 Minutes*) *The Fifth Estate*. Both, like CBC Radio's *As It Happens*, were omnibus or variety shows—shows that juxtaposed various news and arts stories without attempting to connect them. Of the two, *The Fifth Estate* allowed each story the most time and examined it in more depth. In her later television work, Clarkson moved away from news to become an arts host, on *Adrienne Clarkson's Summer Festival* and *Adrienne Clarkson Presents.*

Take 30, filling the 3:30-to-4:00 p.m. time slot, began in 1961 as a show primarily for women. Each day of the week was devoted to a particular subject: entertainment, household advice, public affairs, men's taste, and travel. By 1964, when Clarkson joined the program as its book reviewer, the focus was broader and less systematic. In 1967, *Maclean's* described *Take 30* as, "relentlessly educational, on topics ranging from cooking through politics, architecture, university life, and the new theology" (Dingman). There was still, however, a strong focus on women's issues, sexual views and practices, the emergence of feminism, and the contemporary family.

When Clarkson became co-host in 1965, much of her time was spent interviewing guests associated with women's issues and the arts. Although most of the interviews she conducted were for information purposes, designed to introduce guests and their ideas to the audience rather than challenge or discredit their views, many of them involved controversial issues and issues relating to social conscience. *Maclean's*, in 1973, commented, "If there is a social problem anywhere in the world, *Take 30* will be there, full of concern. It's a guilt-ridden old show which is sloppily produced and suicidally depressing" (Robertson).

Melinda McCracken, in her 1972 *Maclean's* article, noted that Clarkson had recently interviewed Buckminster Fuller, Conor Cruise O'Brien, Sir Kenneth Clark, Spike Milligan, Arthur Koestler, and possibly Edward Albee. That year, Clarkson also interviewed Stanley Kramer regarding his difficulties in financing such politically charged films as *Judgment at Nuremburg* and *Guess Who's Coming to Dinner*. She occasionally did a series of interviews for the show, such as her conversations with thirteen anonymous husbands on the topic of marriage, which she published in 1971 as the book *True to You in My Fashion*. In 1967, she interviewed poet and novelist Leonard Cohen; they talked about how he'd taken up folksinging. In an essay she published in 2000, Clarkson admits that this interview was especially soft-edged because she was in awe of her subject: "Leonard said to me softly, and with only the slightest hint of irony, 'The time is over Adrienne, when poets sit on marble steps wearing long black capes.' The impact on his callow interviewer was such that I could only stare down at my hands, which were plucking at my woollen skirt in an agitated fashion" ("Counterpoint").

The sentimentality evident in many *Take 30* segments arose from the "guilt" identified by *Maclean's* and the show's overt humanism. The people behind the program believed that we all deserve to live in a better world—a world more beautiful, more spiritual, and more just, one in which individuals have a greater chance of enjoying themselves and realizing their aspirations. While the investigative journalism of *The Fifth Estate*, which Clarkson joined at its 1975 launch, had a harder, more sceptical edge than did the informational reporting of *Take 30*, the latter's sentimental humanism was still implicitly present. The title of *The Fifth Estate* alludes to the three estates of early European constitutional law: the clergy, the aristocracy, and the bourgeoisie, to which, in some countries, was eventually added a fourth estate—the working class. Estates are presumed to have a right to political power, and in the British parliamentary system they evolved into the House of Lords (representing the aristocracy and the clergy) and the House of Commons. The term "fifth estate"—or "fourth estate" in some countries—was somewhat presumptuously coined with the emergence of newspapers and journalists in the eighteenth century. It was meant to imply a quasi-governmental role for journalism, presumably an ombudsman role of exposing the activities of the other estates.

The producers of *Take 30* tended to choose as guests people whose lives or ideas might be considered worthy of respect or emulation. But *The Fifth Estate*'s producers often chose people whose values they could challenge or discredit—its journalists soon became known as "the gotcha gang." Implicit in this process, however, was the humanistic assumption that society deserved better than the greed, commercial intimidation, injustice, chicanery, criminal violence, state violence, and civil insurrection that the show documented and investigated; also implicit was the assumption that improvement was possible. Clarkson's contributions included: a program on the McCain family frozen-food empire; several programs on nuclear energy; a program on French-immersion schooling; a series on breast cancer (over which she and producer John Kastner would later quarrel, each claiming to have had the original inspiration); a program on RCMP investigations of Quebec separatism; a segment on novelist Antonine Maillet after she'd won the Prix Goncourt; and international stories such as the Soviet invasion of Afghanistan, the arms trade and sectarian violence in Northern Ireland, and the newly anointed president of Haiti, "Baby Doc" Duvalier.

Clarkson's thoughts during these years are most clearly preserved in the articles she published and in a few print interviews. A recurrent theme is that many people and corporations are too interested in profit, and that material goals should only be sought as part of a compromise with aesthetic, cultural, spiritual, and environmental ideals. Reflected in this theme are the late-nineteenth-century ideas of Matthew Arnold on an emerging conflict between people of "culture" and materialist "philistines," their revision in the 1930s by F.R. Leavis into a struggle between "the cultivated person" and "mass culture," and their more poetic dissemination at the University of Toronto during the 1960s by Northrop Frye. Frye described an opposition between a dominant, anarchic, and amoral "world of the tiger" and a fragile world of human creativity that, at best, could cast a "shadow" over chaos: "The world we see and live in, and most of the world we have made, belongs to the alienated and absurd world of the tiger. But in all our efforts to imagine or realize a better society, some shadow falls across it of the child's innocent vision of the impossible created world that makes human sense" (*Modern Century* 121).

Clarkson's writing frequently constructs such oppositions between material development and imagination, between mere "brutal power" and human "cherishing," and it urges some mixing of the two. Writing of visiting Canada's "sacred" Arctic in 1972, she proclaimed, "If we could refuse the act of domination, the act of brutal power, then conservation and development could be seen in their proper relationship to one another, integrated into a larger plan which emphasizes cherishing and not exploitation" ("If It's Sunday"). Also in 1972, she published a satirical report, called "Ecological Chic," on the opulence of a United Nations conference on the environment. She wrote about the "enormous smorgasbord" that was served to delegates and journalists, a feast that she clearly saw as belonging more to Frye's world of the greedy and amoral tiger than to the "cherishing" world of the ecologist: "More food than even 3,000 people could eat weighted the tables. As mountains of smoked reindeer, marinated salmon, poached snow grouse and tiny prawns were consumed, much discussion took place about the division that was beginning to appear at the conference between the rich and poor nations."

Her satire here was directed at activists and journalists ("one had the feeling that the . . . conference was only an excuse for a giant love-in of the ecologically converted and an intellectual meat market for journalists seeking stories"); official speakers, like Shirley Temple Black, who "announced that she eats only organic foods, rides a bicycle and is against useless over-packaging"; and American delegates who "became misty-eyed at the very thought . . . that .7% of the gross national product of the rich counties should be spent to help the poor counties."

Later, Clarkson expressed these reservations about the spiritual and creative poverty of material wealth more personally, telling Sandra Martin in 1988 that she believed in "a union of the spiritual and the material that gives a meaning to life that goes beyond earning a dollar and reaching for rungs on the ladder." She also told Martin that she had moved from broadcasting to being Ontario's agent general in Paris to being publisher of McClelland and Stewart not for money but because of her "deep concern for Canadian culture." In 1991, she again spoke publicly about the North and its incompatibility with materialism, arguing that Canada is a northern nation, and that "over the last 25 years, the search for material goods has deflected what is basic and decent." "Canada was never about just making money," she wrote, "it was about creating a truly new country based on two cultural groups, the French and the English, and enriching it with adventurous people from other nations" ("Are We Selling Out?"). Of course, unlike many Canadians, Clarkson has led a privileged life. She hasn't had to struggle to earn a living; and (unlike her own father) she could afford "adventure" without financial risk.

Another closely related early theme for Clarkson was that Canada is a "noble" country because it is bilingual and multicultural—a "funny, gigantic, mutant hybrid . . . with the noble aspiration of a bilingual country" she called it in a 1979 Opinion Platform column for the *Financial Post*. A few years later, in an address to the Canadian Bar Association, she maintained that Canadians, and Canadian lawyers, were ideally positioned to take part in the new global economy, "because we are a bilingual, multicultural country" ("Paris Memo"). From that statement, she moved easily to the declaration of another national characteristic: "we are, by record, one of the most decent peoples in the world." In a 1997 article entitled "Immigration, As It Should Be," she remarked with more restraint that Canada is a "place renowned for its tidy orderliness, its sullen decency, its violent climate. A place with parliamentary democracy, English common law, the Napoleonic code, officially bilingual in two major European-origin languages, and with a relationship to the land and nature embodied in its indigenous peoples."

The themes of northernness and decency have often merged in Clarkson's thought. This pairing has also circulated in mainstream Canadian culture, at least since the fiction of Ralph Connor, the poetry of E.J. Pratt and F.R. Scott, and the Arctic paintings of Lawren Harris. Clarkson, however, gives the concept of northern decency a particular social twist. She first articulated this clearly in 1991, in the short *Homemaker's Magazine* essay "Are We Selling Out?": "We have a northern character. Based on both the disadvantages and the advantages of toughing it out in a cold climate. I think of it this way. Someday I might be out there in 40-below weather. I'll be freezing and I'll have to knock on the door of strangers and they'll have to take me in. The knowledge that nature is greater than we are has shaped our character and made us a people who understand that not everyone is responsible for their own misfortunes . . . We worked long and hard for many years to gain the kind of social security we have for everyone in the country. We know it is a difficult country to live in, and we have always had a general understanding among us that we had to help each other, because otherwise we couldn't make this country work at all."

After her appointment as governor general, Clarkson returned to this idea, telling *Klondike Sun* reporter Dan Davidson during an official visit to Dawson City, "The time has come now when we have to state—that we are a society which really doesn't expect everyone to be a winner, doesn't expect everybody to do well monetarily and pay for everything that they do. Here in the Yukon you do understand that if you're going to live in a climate like this you have to have help." Two months later, in addressing a Canadian studies conference, she said that northern Dene and Inuit communities knew "100 per cent . . . that they had to help each other in that climate, on that ice, or perish. And that's what a lot of Canada is about" (archived speech, 16 May 2000). Clarkson's sentimental portrayal of the Dene and Inuit as benevolent socialists is difficult to square with records such as the journals of eighteenth-century explorer Samuel Hearne, who witnessed murderous enmity between the two peoples. But it does help create a national myth.

Over the years, Clarkson has paid much less attention to women's issues than she has to questions about Canada, its northernness, and the general qualities of its culture. Yet the media has indirectly framed her as a powerful woman or a model of female success—an example of the kind of woman feminist movements should produce. The various surveys of influential women or mothers published by *Chatelaine* in the 1970s and 1980s invariably included Clarkson. Her image, in such publications and elsewhere, was usually that of the self-made woman, the immigrant child who had made her way by excelling at school and college. This wonder woman had soared to television stardom on the strength of her dedication to hard work, her intelligence, her beauty, and her amazing ability to multi-task. Her example implied that women could be both chatelaines and career women, and that society did not necessarily restrain a woman's ambition.

It was in a 1970 *Chatelaine* survey of "a cross section of prominent Canadian women" entitled "Do We Need Women's Lib?" that Clarkson made her first comments on feminism. She dissociated herself from feminist political groups on the grounds that liberation "has to do essentially with individual liberty and the compromise that such liberty must make with . . . society." She went on to profess her support for "equal pay for equal work," "the possibility of recruitment and promotion in large corporations," and the repeal of any law suggesting "that a woman is not solely responsible for her life, her property, and her social relationships." In the context of the comments of the other "prominent" women included in the survey, none of these views were especially radical. Clarkson also urged "a change in personal attitudes of women themselves. They must learn to have a sense of personal dignity and an idea of their own worth." This remark was very close to saying, "Shape up, ladies! Your difficulties are your own fault." All of her remarks were consistent with a liberal feminist position that resisted radical and systemic social change and upheld the notion that a few regulatory changes would permit ambitious women to become lawyers, doctors, broadcasters, and company directors.

Such, of course, was not the view of most feminists of the period. They quite rightly insisted that the barriers to women's success were systemic and could only be removed by collective or political action, not by individual initiative. Interestingly, Clarkson's 1968 and 1970 novels betray the author's curiosity about the position of women in a systemically "puritan" Canadian society, and about sexual freedom. *Hunger Trace*, in particular, implies that a woman who claims her sexual freedom may seriously disrupt the hypocrisies on which many marriages are based and the patriarchal club values of Canada's political parties. Her 1971 book of interviews with men on the subjects of love, sex, adultery, and marriage, *True to You in My Fashion*, indirectly addressed the situation of the women in these men's lives and showed that the women were constrained by the men's collective attitudes.

Clarkson's rare remarks on such matters in the later 1970s also demonstrate such an awareness. In her 1979 Opinion Platform article, she alluded sarcastically to politicians who believe that woman's goals have been fulfilled now that she opens doors for herself and "lights her own Virginia Slims." Mocking the social significance of her own CBC television success, she wrote, "Women are on the national news as reporters, and all's right with the world." She went on to deplore the unfairness to women inherent in the Canada Pension Plan and the fact that the affirmative-action Outreach job-creation program had made women ineligible for assistance.

However, Clarkson did not, like many women of the time, attempt to define herself through such concerns. As Melinda

McCracken, who interviewed Clarkson in 1972, explained, "she speaks out about taking the abortion law out of the Criminal Code every chance she gets, but . . . [she says] if women want the abortion law repealed they'll have to go after their MPs." McCracken found this to be "a strange attitude: here is a powerful woman who, if she went out on a limb, might go a long way towards accomplishing what she advocates"; she then reflected that Clarkson seemed "more interested in feelings and insights into women's problems than in the issues." McCracken also observed that Clarkson acted in what—during that era—appeared to be nonfeminist ways. In McCracken's judgement, Clarkson was overly concerned about her makeup and couturier clothing, implying a regressive desire to create herself as an attractive sexual object. Clarkson also appeared to her interviewer insufficiently embarrassed by the fact that she and her husband, Stephen, employed a female housekeeper. This led McCracken to ask herself, "How can you edit books on women's lib when your freedom to do so is bought at another woman's expense?" But the real justice question here, which McCracken failed to pose, was whether Clarkson was paying the housekeeper an appropriate or an exploitative wage.

Between 1985 and her acceptance of the governor generalship in 1999, Clarkson published very little social commentary. Her public statements during her years as agent general for Ontario in France (1982 to 1986) were, for the most part, confined to her job. Her CBC Television work on *Adrienne Clarkson's Summer Festival* (the summers of 1988 and 1989) and its successor, *Adrienne Clarkson Presents*, was far closer to cultural promotion than critical commentary. Of necessity, an arts or variety entertainment host presents artists and performers whose work he or she endorses and wishes others to see. "Wonderful, wonderful,"

Ed Sullivan would enthuse as performers on his archetypal variety show took their bows. All the while, he'd urge the audience to applaud. Cheerleading is the appropriate role for the arts host, and perhaps it's also appropriate training for a governor general.

Clarkson's shows focused mainly on Canadian entertainers who were unknown to mainstream audiences and who reflected what might be called Canadian "diversity." On *Summer Festival,* she featured such performers as Saskatchewan singer and children's entertainer Brenda Baker; Calgary songwriter, folksinger, and social activist James Keelaghan; and Celtic singer Loreena McKennitt—presenting them all early in their careers. In 1989, during the show's second season, she aired a special on Leonard Cohen, profiles of Mario Vargas Llosa, Donald Sutherland, Karen Kain, Laurence Olivier, and Herbert von Karajan, an interview with John Polanyi, and one with Prince Charles, who spoke on architecture. On *Adrienne Clarkson Presents,* she offered a portrait of Vincent Van Gogh, a history of the Downchild Blues Band, profiles of ballerina Veronica Tennant, painters Paterson Ewen, Attila Lukacs, and Don Maynard, tenors Ben Heppner and Richard Margison, figure skater Gary Beacom, jazz musician Randy Raine-Reusch, puppeteer Ronnie Burkett, video artist Paul Wong, the female country-music group Quartette, composer Victor Davies, installation artist Diana Thorneycroft, photographer Freeman Patterson, pianist Jon Kimura Parker, the satiric singing group Moxy Fruvous, blues singer Jodie Drake, playwrights Richard Harrison and Michel Tremblay, architect Arthur Erickson, and novelist Rohinton Mistry. She also produced a highly publicized profile of the Italian Renaissance painter Artemisia Gentileschi, which focused on the attempt of her father and a suitor to force her into marriage through rape. Except, perhaps, for the profiles of Parker, Tremblay, and Tennant, and for a program on bringing Michael Ondaatje's novel *The English Patient* to the screen, Clarkson's shows again featured relatively obscure Canadian artists whom she wanted to see gain wider recognition. A pervasive theme in all this was the diversity of Canadian culture in terms of its artistry, racial origin, and international appeal. "We've got a variety and a richness now, which is phenomenal," she told Martin Morrow in 1992. "And it's coming from every region of the country."

I mentioned earlier that as chair of the Canadian Museum of Civilization from 1995 to 1999, a position that included responsibility for the Canadian War Museum, Clarkson supported the inclusion of a Holocaust gallery as a major part of a new War Museum building. This enraged many veterans and the people at *Esprit de Corps* magazine. The stand she took on this issue was consistent with her well-known stand on ethnic diversity and the international expression of Canadianness. It was also, perhaps, reflective of her naivety about how narrow and ungenerous the views of other Canadians can be, and how risky it can be to generalize about humanity. In a foreword that she wrote to a 1999 book copublished by the Museum of Civilization, *Celebrating Inuit Art: 1948–70,* she spoke warmly of that art as a "joyful celebration of myth and legend . . . that speaks to us all, for it speaks in the voice of elemental human concerns, beliefs, and aspirations." For Clarkson, Inuit art was not only transcendently human but also quintessentially Canadian: "It is an art that evokes the spiritual essence of a country like Canada—and our intrinsic loneliness in the face of a landscape that is vast, often empty, often unknowable. It might be this, above all, that makes Inuit art so evocative of what it means to be Canadian—and perhaps, at heart, what it means to be human." Later that year, in a foreword to an essay collection called *L.M. Montgomery and*

Canadian Culture, she made similar generalizations about the generosity of Canadians. In Montgomery's *Anne of Green Gables,* she suggested, Matthew and Marilla's adoption of Anne, which allows them to be "loved by someone outside their 'family,'" is "a metaphor for Canada as a country that receives immigrants." The novel, Clarkson wrote, confirms her own childhood experience of "the decency and kindness of Canadians—both French and English speaking."

The speech-act theorist John L. Austin makes a distinction between statements that report a previous or existing condition or fact (constative statements), and those that are "speech acts"— statements that attempt to bring a condition or situation into being by speaking it (performative statements). The most obvious performative statements are the ones used in marrying, christening, or the opening or adjourning of meetings, when a statement of a fact or an action—"I now declare you man and wife"— makes it so. Statements such as promises, wishes, warnings, or orders are also performative. Clarkson's statements that Inuit art is "joyful" and that Canadians possess "decency and kindness" are best understood not as constative statements of fact but as performative statements of desire—like the hockey cheers "Go Leafs Go!" or (more appropriate to Clarkson) "Go Canada Go!" That is, the ideas they put forward are not about the Canada that exists but about a Canada that could be, a Canada that the act of making the statement could bring into being.

Since she took on the role of governor general, Clarkson's public utterances have become increasingly performative or cheerleading in tone, most likely because the genre of a given occasion—an awards ceremony, the dedication of a building, a congratulatory address to a graduating class—requires it. Almost every Clarkson speech begins with, "I am delighted," "I'm very happy," "I'm really happy," "It is my great pleasure," "It's very moving," "It's truly a pleasure," "It's a wonderful chance," "It's wonderful to be here," "What a pleasure," "I want to give the very warmest of welcomes," "What a glorious morning," "I am pleased," "I'm so pleased," or some other upbeat declaration. These, presumably, are perceived by Clarkson as part of the rhetoric of the occasion or the viceregal function. She employs the word "wonderful" in many of her opening sentences, and in most speeches she uses it, or an equivalent—"marvellous," "terrific," "glorious"—within her first sequence of sentences.

In her installation speech, delivered to the combined houses of Parliament, she repeatedly congratulated Canada and Canadians on their successes—on their "evolution and constant reaffirmation," their "four centuries of give-and-take, compromise and acceptance," their "notorious decency" and "infamous desire to do good," their "beauty and excellence." These qualities, she asserted, belonged to every Canadian since the aboriginal peoples and the earliest European explorers "dreamed life into being." Contemporary Canadians, especially recent immigrants, have continued this dreaming. Clarkson urged Canadians to see their country as "an old experiment, complex and, in worldly terms, largely successful," and themselves not "as a people to whom things are done but as people who do things." She illustrated this upbeat view with references to her family's reception in Canada and her positive experiences as a child in Canadian public schools. She made allusions not only to the eighteenth-century explorers that are a standard part of Canadian history but also to popular authors such as Farley Mowat and Michael Ondaatje, giving her exhortations the credibility of literacy and historical knowledge.

Those who commented publicly on this speech tended to be

equally excessive in their rhetoric. "'I thought the speech was a knockout,' said novelist Margaret Atwood, a longtime friend of Ms. Clarkson's," Richard Foot of the *National Post* reported ("Embark"). "Hail to thee, blithe Adrienne Clarkson," sang a *Globe and Mail* editorial. "Your installation speech, so sweetly literate and evocative, quite pleased us" ("Thank You"). The *Globe*'s allusion to the Romantic poet Shelley, who wrote that poets are the world's "unacknowledged legislators," correctly identified the ideological ancestry of her optimism. "Clarkson's inaugural speech . . . was a humdinger. It had people talking for days," wrote Norma Greenaway in the *Vancouver Sun*. Greenaway also repeated the *Ottawa Sun*'s comment that the speech was "touchingly personal, literate, and profound."

In most of Clarkson's speeches, there are a number of repeated and interlocking ideas. One is the humanistic notion that the human spirit is much the same everywhere and that nourishing it is our deepest need. Furthermore, it is art that provides the necessary nourishment and teaches us the universality of our feelings. The human spirit is positive and creative, and it spawns the national and immigrant "dreams" and the "stirring of imaginative curiosity" that Clarkson celebrated in her installation speech. "The performers change what might have been personal and private in your own imaginations, in your own emotions— your own sense of isolation, anger, love beauty, joy—into something universal," Clarkson told her audience at the presentation ceremony for the 2000 Governor General's Performing Arts Awards (archived speech, 3 Nov. 2000). In general, her speeches have a discontinuous sound-bite quality of briefly developed and quickly abandoned images or ideas held together by a vocabulary of excitement, pleasure, or admiration and repeated allusions to historic or literary names.

As one would expect, given Clarkson's English literature training, she makes frequent mention of the role of literature in culture and often quotes literary texts. She regularly refers to her undergraduate years at Trinity College and to the views and values she acquired there. These views are mostly the romantic, nationalist, and Arnoldian humanist ones of the late nineteenth century, as elaborated by Leavis and Frye. In this belief system, the traditions of literature and of art in general replace religion as the location of the spiritual. Clarkson's comments on her education and on art and literature are usually expressed in a religious vocabulary of spiritual illumination. During a University of Toronto convocation address, she recalled her years at Trinity as being "fuelled by the classic liberal approach to education," which showed her the "brilliance . . . of the past, like stars that reach us through so many years with their light. What had been written and lived, and what we currently lived, were part of one shining band, a path illuminated like a kind of Milky Way to the future." Her teachers at Trinity, she said, especially Arthur Barker and Northrop Frye, "gave me . . . deep respect for literature, for the creative imagination and the effort of human beings to light a beacon for what can be good, beautiful, and true in life" (archived speech, 19 June 2001).

Accordingly, to Clarkson, literature and debates about what is literary do not reflect social conflict, or particular social contentions, as most contemporary literary theorists assume. Instead, they reflect indisputable universal and eternal human values. "Literature gives us a kind of moral compass," she claimed in presenting the 2001 Governor General's Awards for Literature, "speaking to the moral imperative of humanity by identifying standards and values rooted in eternities rather than in this particular time" (archived speech, 14 Nov. 2001).

By embracing this understanding of literature, Clarkson has at her disposal a roster of authors whom she can interpret as writing to affirm spiritual values—the "great names" of English and world literature. In her speeches, she calls on a much smaller group of these names than she does in her two novels. She refers frequently to John Donne (whose "No man is an island" she has repeated in at least four of her "caring Canadians" speeches so far), William Blake, Jane Austen, the Brontë sisters, W.B. Yeats, and T.S. Eliot; Yeats and Eliot are the most recent international English-language poets of whom she seems aware. She rarely, if ever, quotes American writers. On special occasions, she'll quote a writer who is nationally or locally appropriate to the audience of her speech: Neruda in Chile, Borges in Argentina, German Canadian poet Walter Bauer in Germany, Jose Saramago in welcoming the Portuguese ambassador, Tolstoy and Turgenev in welcoming Russian president Putin, Amos Oz in welcoming the president of Israel, Anne Marriott and Sharon Butala in Regina, Wallace Stegner in Manitoba, Antonine Maillet in New Brunswick. (These occasional references may well be the work of research staff.) Among Canadian writers, she frequently mentions Margaret Laurence ("one of our greatest novelists"), Roch Carrier ("a wonderful writer"), Frye ("one of Canada's greatest writers"), Robertson Davies ("our great writer"), Marshall McLuhan ("one of Canada's greatest thinkers"), and occasionally Harold Innis ("one of our greatest thinkers"), Louis Dudek, Malcolm Ross, and Robert Kroetsch.

By and large, there is not a lot of depth to these references. When she speaks of Laurence, she usually quotes the same line from her autobiography rather than her "great" novels; in her two references to Dudek, she quotes a single line about civilization; and in her several mentions of Ross, she merely cites the title of

his best-known book—*The Impossible Sum of Our Traditions*—
which she tends to get wrong. If she had read much of this book,
which emphasizes unity in diversity, she'd likely have referred to
at least a passage in it. It is only from Frye and McLuhan that
she offers a variety of quotes, although the Frye quotes she
chooses invariably relate to her favourite themes of the spiritual
aspects of art and the universality of humanity and its artistic
and spiritual experiences.

Universal humanity, as Clarkson declared in presenting the
2000 Bravery Awards, is expressed whenever people act selflessly—although presumably it is not expressed when people, as
she lamented at the ceremony, are "motivated solely by selfish-
ness, self-interest, and the pursuit of money." Acts of selflessness
and bravery, Clarkson told the award recipients, "tell us that
people are connected by their common humanity and that
human beings will forfeit self-interest to ensure the well-being
of others, from family members to complete strangers" (archived
speech, 26 June 2000).

Many of Clarkson's speeches emphasize the notion that Canadians are a "caring" and "community-minded" people in many
ways, not just in terms of physical courage. Canadians "have a
history of tolerance and generosity, and of redressing wrongs.
We have learned to balance our individual needs with sharing
the needs of others. And we have, for generation after generation, welcomed strangers," Clarkson told the Forum for Young
Canadians (archived speech, 13 Apr. 2000). There is a Canadian
"tradition" of "concern for others and response to community,"
she told the City of Winnipeg (archived speech, 1 Aug. 2000). In
unveiling a statue of Dr. Norman Bethune, she praised Bethune
for believing in "the welfare of others," for believing that "if we
can't say that we can liquidate poverty and inequalities, then we

must make sure that other things like medical care for people come up to a certain standard to help, to even out those inequalities" (archived speech, 19 Aug. 2000). "Community is the most important thing that human beings can create together[;] because of that sense of community, people realize that they are not alone, that they are not just individuals," she told the village of Minto, New Brunswick (archived speech, 11 Oct. 2000).

Sometimes, her extemporaneous and doctrinaire praise of caring has led her into logical impasses that visibly puzzle her because they expose the politics of her views. She told the Canadian Association of Foodbanks that "All our communities and all our history are filled with stories of helping each other through individual acts of kindness or on the societal scale through public health." But, this spoken, she abruptly found herself unable to ignore the contradiction between her idealistic view of Canada as "caring" and "decent" and the reality that private food-bank initiatives are necessary because Canada's government allows such poverty. "Most of us in this country simply accept, as average Canadians, that we are the best place in the world to live—or so the United Nations indicators tell us," she continued. "But how can we live in the best country in the world and still have food banks? I'd like that to be answered for me. Perhaps some of you might have that answer, or perhaps you ask the same question" (archived speech, 1 June 2001).

Socialists, of course, believe that the fundamental well-being of citizens should be maintained systematically by the nation-state, and not by means of an assortment of private or personal measures that may or may not be enacted. Even adherents of Canadian Red Toryism believe that a well-governed nation-state will be sufficiently "decent" to protect its citizens from penury. It is this nation-state, this "collective," that Clarkson repeatedly characterizes as "decent" and "caring" in a number of her other speeches. In the Foodbanks speech, however, her perplexity in the face of the blunt fact that the nation-state is *not* decent and caring when it comes to minimum food requirements almost brings her confident speech to a baffled halt. Her usual platitudes about Canadian caring are not going to feed people. She realizes that, for once, her idealism does not have the "answer."

A few months later, when opening an exhibit on refugee camps, she encountered a similar moment. After praising the generosity of the French medical organization Médecins Sans Frontières and praising Canada for being "a multicultural bilingual country that seems to work better than almost any country made of these kinds of elements," she found herself recalling the racism that attended her arrival in Canada. "We pride ourselves on being a peaceful, decent, giving people. But there are aspects of our history that we can certainly regret. We have been unjust to whole groups of people in the past—refusing to let refugees, whether Sikhs, or Jews, enter our country, depriving Japanese-Canadians of their human rights, refusing Chinese their civil status. All of this now has changed in a remarkably short time" (archived speech, 28 Sept. 2001). Clarkson's problem here is that she has so often declared Canadians to be "decent" and "caring" in an absolute sense. But the situations she recalls indicate that for most of their history Canadians were anything but. She takes refuge in the speed of the transformation—"All of this now has changed in a remarkably short time." But this speedy transformation also implies that Canadian decency has existed for "a remarkably short time."

For Clarkson, Canadian acts of caring are especially valuable if they are performed through public institutions and are thus closely tied to the nation-state and a caring public policy. It is as if these acts are, for her, mirror images of the historic injustices of the Canadian nation-state—the internment of Japanese Canadians, the rejection of the Sikhs on the *Komagata Maru*, the turning away of the Jews on the *S.S. St. Louis*—and an atonement for them. Her praise of paid public servants is as strong as her praise of volunteers. In presenting the 2000 Public Service Achievement Awards, Clarkson declared that "a strong public service, reflecting a vision of the public good, is a cornerstone upon which Canada was built"; she also claimed that she was nostalgic for her youth, because her generation "believed in public service as one of our highest ideals." She went on to regret that "Today's young people are more likely to worship at the altar of deal-making," that "the chance of making a lot of money can have more appeal . . . than crafting public policy that fosters social well-being" (archived speech, 18 May 2000). Interestingly, this is not a regret that Clarkson has voiced in any of her numerous speeches to high school and university audiences. In presenting the Public Service Awards the following year, her praise became so extravagant that it obscured the fact that public servants are salaried employees, characterizing the winners as "men and women who selflessly dedicate themselves to the service of the nation" (archived speech, 16 Oct. 2001).

Whether civil deficits such as poverty, homelessness, and hunger should be addressed by the state, by corporate and private charity, by volunteer services, or by some other means, is, of course, a political issue. It's also one on which Canada's politicians—often members of the same party—have divergent views. Clarkson, however, attempts to raise this issue above politics by attaching it to transcendent concepts such as "the human spirit" or a "Canadian tradition." After praising the 2001 Public Service Award winners, for example, she went to say that their "exemplary commitment to the ideal of public service" is "what distinguishes us as a nation. It has been said that Canadians have a genius for public enterprise; our commitment to the larger interest, the public good, is fundamental to what it means to be a Canadian." (Here, by using the passive voice—"It has been said"—Clarkson tries to disguise as a commonly spoken statement a view that is most vigorously articulated in her husband's book *Reflections of a Siamese Twin*.)

At the 2000 Governor General's Canadian Study Conference, she encountered some resistance to this kind of strategy. In her conference-opening address, Clarkson, as well as restating her questionable idea that the "northern" aboriginal tradition of helping each other because of the cold climate was "what a lot of Canada is about," said that a "Canadian society which can tolerate 3,000 homeless people in shelters a night in one of its largest cities, of whom 1,000 are children, is not the kind of society which I think we want to sustain in its present state. If you do think it is tolerable, as future influential leaders, then you will be changing Canada profoundly." Then she commented on shelters for abused women, stating that "women who are powerless are more powerless than any man." She quickly added, "That is not a feminist statement, that is simply a fact. The level of resources our society allocates to the needs of abused women is not exemplary. I would like to think more could be done with compassion and understanding so that those who are most powerless, most helpless, and most in need can become part of what we all are as Canadians" (archived speech, 16 May 2000).

Much as she'd done when confronted with the paradox that a "caring" Canada left its poor to the uncertainties of food banks, Clarkson here abruptly demonstrates the confusions and contradictions in her thinking. If Canada were an inherently caring society, if this national quality were indeed one that existed beyond politics and political debate, then the country would not have thousands of homeless people and would not need to be changed from its "present state." Her claim that to find such homelessness "tolerable" would be to change Canada "profoundly" is illogical, since she has already described the "present state" of the country as one in which substantial homelessness is tolerated. Moreover, her assertion that Canada and Canadians are inherently compassionate implies that those who would change Canada in this way are un-Canadian, since they would be moving the country away from its true nature and changing compassion from being an eternal Canadian quality to one that is subject to political decision making.

Clarkson's remarks about women's powerlessness here are similarly troublesome. Canadians should do more for "powerless" women, she implies, because Canada is a compassionate country. But if Canada truly were an intrinsically compassionate country, then Canadians would already be doing whatever was necessary and wouldn't have any powerless women. Moreover, she contradicts herself when she claims that "women who are powerless are more powerless than any man" is not a feminist statement and asserts that it is merely a statement of "fact." The statement is too general to be a statement of fact and too imprecise in its quick shift from powerlessness as an absolute condition ("women who are powerless") to powerlessness as a condition that is relative and comparative because it has degrees ("more powerless"). Furthermore, it is possible to conceive of powerless men—mentally ill, perhaps, and possibly crippled, as well as poor—who are "more powerless" than "powerless" women who are not so afflicted. Since the statement is not one of fact (a constative statement), it is immediately recognizable as a statement of desire (a performative statement), and thus it is immediately evident that the speaker wishes, for ideological reasons, to have her audience mistake it as fact. Aware of this, Clarkson attempts to recoup by adding the qualification that it "is not a feminist statement." But this claim just signals her own realization that it *is* a feminist statement and confirms the perception of any audience member who sees it that way.

In Clarkson's closing address to the conference, she made it clear that there were indeed people in the audience who recognized the statement as political. She revealed that after her opening remarks someone had challenged her view of homelessness: "When a gentleman asked me 'Isn't this political?' all I will say to you is 'Do you know a political party in Canada whose platform said that they are for homelessness and poverty?' No. Therefore, I cannot be the opposition to that. Homelessness and poverty are something that all human beings and all Canadians are against. They are against it because it offends us in our deepest souls as Canadians. And I think that that's why we really have to understand we're not talking about partisan politics. We're talking about humane ideals. We're talking about what people can do for one another, which is why the theme of this conference is so important—the building of communities, and you, yourselves, as future leaders in it."

Whatever we believe about the issue of homelessness—and I personally agree with Clarkson that it is a matter that should be dealt with collectively, through the state—her analysis here is disingenuous in the extreme. Differences between political parties over how homelessness should be addressed—by general economic stimulus, by private charity, by a state-administered guaranteed income, by a state program of public housing—Clarkson reduces to a simple opposition. She implies that anyone who does not endorse attempting to end homelessness through direct state intervention must be in favour of "homelessness and poverty" and therefore lack the "deep souls" of true Canadians. It is a common trick of the rhetorically dishonest to reduce complexities to this kind of simple binary opposition—for example, President George Bush's post-September 11 declaration that anyone who does not support U.S. antiterrorist policies must be a supporter of terrorism.

Many of the other "Canadian" touchstones that Clarkson invokes in her speeches also disguise political issues as nonpolitical ones. Among the words she uses most frequently in her speeches—along with "community," "collective," and "collectivity"—are "diversity" and "inclusiveness," as in, "the inclusiveness we are now so proud of" (archived speech, 4 Aug. 2000). Sometimes, "diversity" becomes "rich diversity" or "glorious diversity," making it clear that it is not a neutral term (archived speeches, 18 Sept. 2000, 20 June 2000). She most often employs these terms in speeches about immigration or the contributions of aboriginal peoples to Canadian culture. Immigration, however, is not currently regarded by all Canadians as an indisputable good, and the government has revised its immigration regulations many times over the past decades. The roles that aboriginal peoples may play in Canadian society have also been a contentious issue, particularly in British Columbia, where most of the land has not been sold or otherwise ceded by aboriginals to the settler populations who occupy it. While people like Clarkson and me may believe that Canadians should be proud of their diversity, to say that they are proud is by no means a nonpolitical statement of fact. It is an obliquely hortatory statement that intervenes politically to urge Canadians to summon up such pride.

In many of her speeches, Clarkson speaks warmly of "public education" and of the fact that she and John Ralston Saul were both educated in public schools. "Universal access to public education," she told a Charlottetown audience, is something "without which no decent democracy can function." It is a "cornerstone of the Canadian egalitarian philosophy. The Fathers of Confederation strongly believed that citizens were created in schools" (archived speech, 27 June). A few days later, in Ottawa, she declared during her Canada Day speech that "Canadian society was built on a commitment to the public good," adding that the Fathers of Confederation "believed strongly in the idea that citizens were created in schools and universal access to public education was a cornerstone of their philosophy." More than a year later, she asked a Berlin audience, "Where do we, as Canadians, learn what it is to be Canadian? . . . It is in public education. Without public education—bearing in mind the mix of all children who come to this country with their parents or who are from the first generation born of immigrant parents—we cannot have a cohesive society of immigrants" (archived speech, 25 Oct. 2001).

During the years of these speeches, some Ontarians were mounting well-organized lobbying efforts to pressure the provincial government to extend public funding to private-non-Catholic religious schools. In late 2001, Premier Mike Harris finally bowed to the pressure. Moreover, several provinces, including Ontario, began sharply reducing their funding to public education. As well, Ontario was drastically curtailing the power of public school boards to create their own programs and manage their own budgets; by the fall of 2002, the province had taken control of the Ottawa, Hamilton, and Toronto boards. In this context, Clarkson's many positive remarks about the value of public education in enabling immigrants to participate in society and in disseminating Canada's "history of great tolerance and great generosity," coupled with the fact that she did not speak at all about various forms of private education, again communicated an implicit political position (archived speech, 8 May 2000).

On one recent occasion, Clarkson's remarks about public education evolved into an open condemnation of religious schools and a seemingly assimilationist endorsement of the public education of immigrant children. Speaking at her alma mater, Trinity College, she regretted the sectarian goals of the college's founder, Anglican bishop John Strachan: "Trinity would [now] be unrecognizable to John Strachan. And just as well. The whole of our modern society in Canada and particularly in Ontario is built now upon the idea of public education which John Strachan's foes fought so hard for . . . Public education is a great glory and something worth fighting for in a country like ours, because without public education we cannot have our kind of democracy. Without education that is public, we cannot integrate immigrants into our values, our way of life and history" (archived speech, 29 Sept. 2001).

As Paula Brook noticed in late 1999, the words and ideas of John Ralston Saul turn up frequently in Clarkson's speeches. Sometimes Clarkson acknowledges these borrowings, as she did when attempting to inject a note of humour into her installation speech: "As John Ralston Saul has written, the central quality of the Canadian state is complexity. It is a strength and not a weakness that we are a permanently incomplete experiment built on a triangular foundation—Aboriginal, Francophone and Anglophone."

Because so many of her speeches require her to speak about Canada, she has borrowed repeatedly—as in the above example—

from Saul's 1997 book *Reflections of a Siamese Twin: Canada at the End of the Twentieth Century* and from his speeches to the Baldwin-Lafontaine Foundation conferences, which he sponsors. In her installation speech alone, in addition to her overt reference to his "triangular foundation" concept, she borrows ideas from him about Canada's age, its history of compromise, and its being a country of "the imagination." Her frequent comments about the "public good" repeat one of the most common phrases in *Reflections*. Her message to Royal Military College cadets that Canada has suffered "only 86 deaths in civil strife in our entire history" is taken from Saul (archived speech, 18 May 2001). Her assertions that Canada is an extremely successful country whose leaders have repeatedly learned to overcome "conflicting interests" through compromise or through working "collectively" is one of the major themes of *Reflections* (archived speech, 8 May 2000). So too is the idea that Canada is a very old country: "I think a lot of people don't even realize that in many ways we are an old country. People say, 'you're such a new country,' but we have one of the oldest constitutions in the world; in the time that we've had the same constitution, France as had five, redrawing all the agreements between themselves as people" (archived speech, 8 May 2000).

In *Reflections,* Saul writes that "Canada is not a new country. In legal terms it is one of the oldest in the world. In constitutional terms it is one of a tiny handful of stable, long-lasting democracies" (13). The observation is so important to him that he repeats it several times—for example: "Canada is now one of the oldest countries in the world, if you take into consideration stable borders and government attached to a peaceful . . . democratic form. It has one of the world's oldest constitutions" (266).

Another staple of Clarkson's speeches (including her installation speech) has been the idea that "Canada is a country, as John Ralston Saul, the writer, has said, 'built on the triangular foundation of Aboriginal, English, and French'" (archived speech, 21 June 2000). Saul's initial phrase for this idea, which appears in the *Reflections* chapter titled "A Triangular Reality," is "a tripartite foundation." He attributes this foundation to Canada's being "constructed upon three deeply rooted pillars, three experiences—the aboriginal, the francophone, and the anglophone" (81). A few months after the June speech, Clarkson restated the idea as her own: "The First Nations people who have been here for the longest are part of a triangular foundation not only of this place, and of this province, but that replicates the foundation of our country, the Aboriginal, the Francophone, and the Anglophone" (archived speech, 10 Oct. 2000).

The next year, she repeated the idea without credit to Saul in four separate speeches. On March 8, she declared that it "has been very important to our national psyche"; she made similar observations on May 7 and on August 20. By the fall of 2001, when she delivered a speech in Berlin, Saul's triangular foundation had not only become her idea but, remarkably, it had also become a normal, accepted idea among Canadians—possibly because Clarkson worked so hard to imprint it on the "national psyche." "Aboriginals," she told her Berlin audience, "passed freely their knowledge of the land and how to live on it to the white-skinned newcomers. This was extremely important in the early history and subsequent evolution of our Canadian society. It is why we say that our society has been built on a triangular base by the Aboriginals, the Francophones and the Anglophones and the influence of these three on each other" (archived speech, 25 Oct. 2001).

The triangular foundation of Canada theory, moreover, depends on a misleading metaphor—a metaphor loosely constructed by Saul that became more and more misleading as Clarkson repeated and simplified it. By the time she spoke in Berlin, she was giving audiences the impression that aboriginal peoples wielded one-third of the influence forming Canadian society. If not an equilateral triangle, Saul's metaphor at least implies a triangle with only roughly similar sides. Clarkson's rhetoric, with its parallel phrases—"the Aboriginals, the Francophones and the Anglophones"—suggests a profound similarity, if not an equivalence, among these sides.

For the Canada of the seventeenth and eighteenth centuries, all possible triangular methods of symbolizing the power of the nation's founding cultures are problematical, partly because few aboriginals were interested in founding a European-style nation, and partly because those who were interested were usually engaged in a subservient relationship to anglophone and francophone enterprise. As the twenty-first century begins, the foundation Saul and Clarkson allude to is made up, according to the most recent census statistics, of an aboriginal population of two percent, a francophone population of twenty-four percent, and an anglophone population of seventy-four percent. Technically, the geometric figure one could draw from these statistics would be a triangle, but it would be a grossly unbalanced one that would illuminate both the swamping of aboriginal culture and its economic weakness as well as the relative fragility of francophone culture. By using the other metaphor that Saul offers in *Reflections* of a Canada "constructed upon three deeply rooted pillars . . . the aboriginal, the francophone, and the anglophone," one could create an equally arresting image of imbalance: the shortest pillar would be only three percent of the height of the tallest. Moreover, to say, as Clarkson did to the Berliners, that Canada was significantly "built" by aboriginals, when indeed it was constructed by settler populations mostly against aboriginals' will, is to blatantly assert a wish in the place of fact.

Clarkson's most recent reworking of this Saul concept was in a speech to the Forum for Young Canadians in which she abandoned the triangle figure and announced that Canada is "based originally on an Aboriginal foundation with English and French added to it. That foundation existed long before the newcomers arrived five hundred years earlier" (archived speech, 14 Mar. 2002). Even more than Saul's triangular foundation theory, this new formulation whitewashes the violent injustices of colonial history. As well as misrepresenting aboriginals as willing participants in white settlement, Clarkson's words evoke the amusing conception of the English and French—far from being illegal immigrants, which is how many of them must have seemed to aboriginals—as legally processed "newcomers" (perhaps "guest workers"?) whom the aboriginals cleverly "added" to their culture.

Clarkson's comments on the importance of public education in inculcating Canadianness in new immigrants have their source in an openly political passage of Saul's *Reflections:* "We have a very unusual, steady, and high level of immigration . . . We cannot invite people in—particularly poor people—and then moan about their effect on our society. If their role is somehow troubling, then it is entirely our fault for not assuming our full responsibilities to smooth the difficult path of immigration. And the primary institutional responsibility is public education . . . This is the most important provincial responsibility . . . By cutting back rather than increasing their education budgets at a time of high immigration, they are not, as they claim, stabilizing their economies. They are destabilizing our society" (440).

Even Clarkson's recurrent comments on how Canada is a "northern" nation and how Canadians tend to forget or overlook that "northernness" have their source in Saul, notably in one of the final chapters of *Reflections,* "The Belt Clingers." In it, he accuses most urban Canadians of clinging to "the belt-line of our southern border" (464). This attitude, he argues, prevents Canadians from developing "an unchallenged northern sense of the sort the Norwegians and the Swedes have . . . The situation is a betrayal both of the north and of the northern ideal" (466–67). As the phrase "the northern ideal" indicates, also present in Saul's view of the north is Clarkson's idealistic notion that it requires social cooperation rather than domination by individuals: "The view of place in northern countries," writes Saul, "is not that of domination or sustained romanticism. What cannot be dominated must be a part of an ongoing coalition" (188).

TAKE SIX

Saulipsisms

OR: The Nonideological Ideologue
More Saulipsisms
Plato's Bastard

What's the difference between a self-construction like Buddhistic, enigmatic Leonard Cohen and a charlatan? A couple of words? Perhaps that's why I thought I had to explain the meaning of *estate*. Up with the press! What are sovereignty and monarchy if not domination? Benevolent ecological despotism? Up with the humanists of the press! Both Adrienne and I have a lot invested in the "notorious decency" of Canadians. All Canadians do, but just because she and John yearn for such decency do we have to love or detest her? I hated myself for weeping at the ends of *The Sound of Music* and *Love Story*. In the 1920s, poet A.J.M. Smith called cultural cheerleading a branch of the Canadian Manufacturers' Association. I kind of wish that Adrienne had managed to be a professional/domestic wonder woman, but I also know that this is probably not a disinterested wish. Smith recommended fewer canoes and less caring in Canadian literature. I'd hate myself for weeping over a reunion of Adrienne and her daughters. Were cheers for Wilson MacDonald like cheers for Leonard Cohen? Has Clarkson ever read an ungreat Canadian novelist? Or met an uncaring Canadian? Sometimes I'd like to "light a beacon" in that grey matter behind Adrienne's eyes, but I try not to say this. It might be read as an allusion to that sexist American poet Robert Creeley. Delightful diversity, I say. It would be helpful if her "moral compass" would show her, and us, some ways through current inequalities. It would be helpful if Clarkson had more subtle spousal ideas to borrow.

> We have always been a middle-class democracy. "Middle-class citizen" has always been the highest real rank we have to offer. There are, of course, those who pretend to be more. (Saul, *Reflections* 468)

Although Saul's ideas about Canada appear to form the basis of most of Clarkson's public statements about Canada and Canadians, these ideas are not in themselves especially coherent or effectively argued. Saul doesn't write nearly as well as Clarkson. When writing nonnarrative prose, he has great difficulty in organizing his thoughts and in signalling the direction of his arguments. His paragraphs are often a series of loosely connected statements and quotations and his chapters a series of loosely linked and partially redundant paragraphs. He will present an idea and then abandon it to present another idea before he has developed, explained, or supported the first. Many of his paragraphs seem like a series of juxtaposed index-card notations—useful, perhaps, as a source of embellishments for public speeches. To compensate for this looseness of argument and organization, Saul repeatedly reiterates or summarizes his arguments—not only at the ends of chapters, but also at transitional points within them. He also characteristically creates very short and specifically titled chapters. These techniques add to the length of his books, but they also make it possible for readers to move quickly from chapter to chapter, or from summary to summary, and to reorient themselves after interrupting their reading.

Perhaps influenced by his investigation of the death of General Ailleret, Saul tends towards conspiracy theories of knowledge. He also tends to construct himself, like his protagonist Stone, as tilting at windmills vastly more powerful than he is, only to be chastised or persecuted by the windmill operators. All of his nonfiction books construct a huge, vaguely menacing idea or set of ideas. He asserts that these ideas are powerful among society's elites and only he can effectively discredit them and bring them to public consciousness. When his nonfiction books meet with criticism, he protests that powerful people dislike or fear him because he has dared to speak out against them.

Saul first reacted in this manner to the criticism of his doctoral thesis supervisors. Dismissing their reservations about his methodology, Saul told John Lownsbrough, "It was a power play, basically. I didn't behave like a student." He had a similar answer when Lownsbrough mentioned the negative reviews of *Voltaire's Bastards*: "To the extent that *Voltaire's Bastards: The Dictatorship of Reason in the West* was reviewed by ideologues, or what I would call mediocre frightened academics, it would be hated because it was profoundly anti-ideological." In 1986, when his novels had met with popular acclaim in Europe but had attracted little attention for their literary merit in North America, Saul proclaimed that the "Western literary elites" who praise Philip Roth and Saul Bellow instead of John Ralston Saul are "degenerates" who "will disappear." He went on to dismiss Booker Prize-winning novelist Anita Brookner as "an insult to the human mind" (Cannon).

As a cultural critic, Saul is a modernist. In the tradition of T.S. Eliot, who attributed twentieth-century materialism to a "dissociation of sensibility" that occurred sometime in the seventeenth century, or of Ezra Pound, who attributed it to the establishment of money-lending during the Italian Renaissance, Saul seeks in *Voltaire's Bastards* a crucial determinative moment in Western history. This moment can be blamed for contemporary culture's high valuation of utilitarian ethics and managerial skills (what Saul variously calls "managerialism" or, more obscurely, "corporatism") and the numerous social, economic, and political deficits this valuation has caused. Some of Saul's reviewers have pointed out that others have made attempts to locate the source of twentieth-century managerialism. Socialist and anarchist-theorist George Woodcock did not mention Eliot or Pound, but he noted that Saul's theory had been anticipated in the 1940s by James Burnham's *The Managerial Revolution* (1941) and George Orwell's *1984* (1949). Marxist social critic Stan Persky noted that Saul had been anticipated by Theodor Adorno and Max Horkheimer's *Dialectic of Enlightenment* (1944). To these a reviewer could have added R.H. Tawney's *Religion and the Rise of Capitalism* (1926) or Jacques Ellul's *L'empire du non-sens: L'art et la société technicienne* (1980). But to give Saul his due, no book on the philosophic origins of managerialism and the rule of technocrats or "technicians" had been written for a popular audience—the *Calgary Sun*, not inappropriately, printed its review of *Voltaire's Bastards* beside a review of a new volume of Yorkshire veterinarian stories by James Herriot.

The kind of amateur historical search that Eliot, Pound, and Saul undertake for a "magic moment" in cultural history when crucial determinations are made and conditions are irremediably altered for the worse, lends itself to highly selective documentation and extreme generalization. Implicit in Woodcock's mention of Burnham and Persky's of Adorno and Horkheimer was the suggestion that the analyses of these theorists had been more careful, comprehensive, subtle, and nuanced than Saul's. Most recent scholarly considerations of the questions Saul asks about the origins of contemporary managerialism have also avoided both simplistic explanation and blame. They have instead suggested that the sources of technocratic thought were part of a large shift in language usage and cultural assumptions that began to occur over a broad area of Europe during the thirteenth and fourteenth centuries. In his multivolume investigation of the "archaeology" of knowledge (*Madness and Civilization*, 1961; *The Order of Things*, 1966; *The Archaeology of Knowledge*, 1969; and *Discipline and Punishment*, 1975)—an examination of the shifting fashions in what cultures view as knowable and valuable to know—Michel Foucault has described such shifts as being from one "episteme," or understanding of knowledge, to another. For example, in one episteme, social deviance may be understood as the consequence of sin, and a society will create institutions for exorcism, confession, repentance, and forgiveness; in a later episteme, deviance may be understood as criminality, and a society will create justice systems, courthouses, prisons, and processes such as bail, parole, and probation. Timothy Reiss, in another large study, *The Discourse of Modernism* (1982), sees what he christens the "analytico-referential" discourse of science, commerce, and managerialism emerging as part of a "paradigm shift" that began in Europe in the late-medieval period. Such epistemic or paradigm shifts, according to theorists like Foucault, Reiss, and Thomas Kuhn—who, in *The Structure of Scientific Revolutions* (1962), first presented the concept of paradigm shift—are attributable to various material and social changes, are a continuing process, and contain the possibility for dissent, especially when they are understood.

Saul's notion that the "abuse" of reason in the late eighteenth century had led to the "soulless" management of Western culture in the twentieth century by managerially trained technocrats may have been a new one to the popular audience for whom he wrote *Voltaire's Bastards*. However, it had been well known, in various more subtle and less emotionally charged forms, in the scholarly community, at least since the work of Tawney in the 1920s, Burnham, Adorno, and Horkheimer in the 1940s, and of Foucault in the 1960s. Apart from a brief reference to Tawney, Saul gives no indication that he is aware that these ideas have been in circulation. Readers are entitled to say to Saul, as Prospero says sardonically to his daughter Miranda in Shakespeare's *The Tempest,* when she declares excitedly that she has discovered a "new" world, "Tis new to thee." However, presenting himself as the solitary critic, as the only one who dares, or has dared, to be knowledgeable, has been part of Saul's self-image—and part of the image he has tried to present to his public—since he presented his doctoral thesis and investigated the death of General Ailleret. Is this self-presentation a deceit? The tone of excited discovery in his books suggests that it may not be. Still, like an image, the tone of a text can also be manufactured. And, ever since experiencing difficulties with his doctoral thesis, Saul has chosen to pitch his "philosophical" works almost exclusively to audiences insufficiently well read to evaluate or challenge them.

Voltaire's Bastard's is representative of Saul's nonfiction. Like Miranda, it is excited and passionate in tone, and it presents perceptions it claims no one has had, or has dared to have, before. Like Clarkson's speeches, it is studded with brief quotations from various writers. And like a television news program, it has a short attention span, moving restlessly from one perception to another and leaving most undeveloped and unsubstantiated. The brief quotations buttress a number of Saul's arguments but are not presented as part of a general discussion of the topics he considers, so that the reader is left unaware of the existence of other opinions that counter or qualify those Saul has cited. Because they are fragmentary, most of the quotations provide little if any understanding of the context in which the statement was made, and little assurance that Saul has read the full text— the Koran, a book by Burke, Baudelaire, or Pascal—that he has cited. With his passionate tone, however, and his frequent creation of narrative—for example, his four-page summary of the Second World War—Saul urges the reader to believe on the basis of the dramatic creation of his own apparently passionate belief.

Saul's thesis is that the form of reason offered by the eighteenth-century French philosopher Voltaire as an antidote to the arbitrariness of an absolute monarchy was bastardized by its inheritors during the French Revolution, divorced from the humanistic values Voltaire believed it should express, and reduced to an overvaluation of organization and bureaucracy for its own sake. Among the results of this are the ineffective, unimaginative, self-interested military bureaucracies that lose the Battle of France in 1940 and murder General Ailleret in 1964 in *The Birds of Prey,* the amoral and unimaginative MBA graduates in *Baraka,* and the curators of *The Next Best Thing,* who operate their museums for their own comfort and profit. Much of *Voltaire's Bastards* consists of additions to the examples of narrow managerialism offered in Saul's novels. These examples derive from literary celebrity, economic policy, foreign policy, and military strategy. Saul has claimed that his work is "nonideological," but it is fairly obvious that most of the targets of his book are politically on the right—from the anti-Semitic French general Weygrand of World War II to Walt Disney and America's Vietnam-era secretary of defence and World Bank president Robert McNamara.

Saul's subsequent books, *The Doubter's Companion* (1994), *The Unconscious Civilization* (1995) *Reflections of a Siamese Twin* (1997), and *On Equilibrium* (2001), rework the central idea of *Voltaire's Bastards,* which is itself a reworking of the insight into military managerialism that Saul had in the 1970s when investigating the Ailleret murder. *The Doubter's Companion* reshapes many the insights of *Voltaire's Bastards* into encyclopaedia form, as brief, alphabetized entries. Some commentators, such as Doug Fetherling in his 1997 article "Citizen Saul," read *The Doubter's Companion* as a simplification and popularization of *Voltaire's Bastards*, but its alphabetical organization may have merely been Saul's acknowledgement that his limited organizational skills had muffled many of *Voltaire's* arguments. The book contains many of the dictionary entries that one might expect: "Business Schools," "Canada," "Corporatism," "Global Economy," "Manager," "Public Education," "Reason," "Voltaire." For the critical tone of *Voltaire's Bastards,* however, Saul tries to substitute irony, and occasionally sarcasm. Many of his unexpected topics are ironic, such as "Happy Birthday," which he employs as a pretext for condemning the commercialization of everyday life, or "Penis," which he uses to condemn the evaluating of politicians by the quality of their sexual relationships. The latter entry, in which he attacks the popular belief that the semen of public figures should not be "expended in other than a legally sanctioned vagina" (230), is now even more ironic than he may have hoped, considering his and Clarkson's hasty marriage on the eve of her appointment as governor general. He also produces more irony than he may have intended in his entry for "Class" (which, like many privileged people, he claims has "never existed in North America"). He remarks that the "basic rule for men seeking social promotion through marriage is to ignore titles, manners and houses until they have clearly established whether the lady is sweeping her way down the stairs or up" (62). Adrienne was definitely ascending.

Two of Saul's dictionary entries appear deliberately false and misleading. His entry for "Ideology" begins with the definition, "Tendentious arguments which advance a world view as absolute truth in order to win and hold political power." He then implies that ideologies are consciously embraced and disseminated. Both sociological and psychological research, however, have repeatedly demonstrated that people's basic ideological assumptions—about the good, about the ethical, about desirable or undesirable cultural practices—are absorbed or formulated during childhood from an array of what Raymond Williams has described as "emergent," "dominant," and "residual" practices and values. Exactly which ones are absorbed depends mostly on the class, region, ethnicity, race, nation-state, and material circumstances into which a person is born, what values are emerging, dominant, or residual in that context, what values the person becomes familiar or comfortable with, and what conditions a culture needs to explain to itself. Ideology is a practical psychological necessity to every person and society because, as Louis

Althusser has observed, it is through the unconscious fundamental assumptions of ideology that people are "formed, transformed, and equipped to respond to the demands of the conditions of their existence" (*For Marx* 235).

For example, one of the major ideologies associated with the United States is the belief that the U.S. is the most ethical country in the world and is therefore obliged to show the world the way to democracy and freedom. This "beacon on the hill" view—which most Americans accept without questioning and which has the practical function of explaining to them their national wealth and cultural distinctness—is much more likely to be absorbed by people who were born in the United States. It is more likely to be absorbed by a white American than one of another race. It is less likely to be absorbed by someone born into an educated family whose members have become conscious of the belief and its limitations.

Similarly, the belief that French racial purity is important and that "impure blood" is fit only to water the fields, as "La Marseillaise" declares in its concluding lines, had cultural practicality when France was being threatened by English, Austrian, Italian, and Spanish enemies in the late eighteenth century. In this era of nonwhite immigration, it has renewed cultural practicality to poorly educated white French citizens who need to explain their poverty or unemployment. These days, it is much more likely to be absorbed by someone who has been repeatedly made to sing that anthem than by someone who grew up elsewhere, singing a different song. It becomes a visible, articulate, and conscious ideology when proclaimed by ambitious right-wing politicians.

One of the reasons that strong, rationally argued ideological beliefs such as the "pure French" nationalist beliefs of Jean-Marie

Le Pen—beliefs that advance a world view as absolute truth in order to gain and hold political power—are difficult to argue against is that they rely on much deeper unconscious ideological assumptions. The examples Saul presents in *The Doubter's Companion* of blameworthy ideologies—ideologies that he implies people would abandon if they would just shape up, think, and become "nonideological" like him—are religious beliefs in exclusive truth, Marxist beliefs about class warfare, group beliefs in racial or national superiority, and economic beliefs in unregulated or globalized markets: "A god who intervenes in human affairs through spokesmen who generally call themselves priests; a king who implements instructions received from God; a predestined class war which requires the representatives of a particular class to take power; a corporatist structure of experts who implement truth through fact-based conclusions; a racial unit which because of its blood-ties has a destiny as revealed by nationalist leaders; a world market which, whether anyone likes it or not, will determine the shape of every human life, as interpreted by corporate executives—all of these and many more are ideologies" (169). To Saul, these are all "naive obsessions" and are therefore distinct from his own beliefs, which he assumes are consciously held and therefore not naive and or ideological.

However, specific overt ideological positions such as these—that God should rule through divinely inspired leaders, that wealthy classes will not voluntarily share with the poor, that a nation such as the United States has a "manifest destiny," that a globalized economy would most efficiently and fairly distribute global wealth—rest on much less specific unconscious assumptions about how the world came into being, how peoples came into being, how human beings behave towards one another, of how friendly, unfriendly, or desperate day-to-day life may be.

Althusser's famous definition of ideology as a representation of "the imaginary relationship of individuals to their real conditions of existence" stresses the imaginary and hypothetical nature of ideology: that it is an unconscious, subliminal working hypothesis about the general conditions of life (*Lenin* 162). This working hypothesis enables people to make more conscious decisions, such as whether mullahs should govern a country, whether abortion should be legal, whether McDonald's restaurants are a good thing, whether immigration should be strictly regulated, whether American-made films are culturally corrupting, whether doctors should be employees of the state, or whether medical care should be provided on a free-enterprise model.

Saul's contention that his views are nonideological, is, of course, nonsense. It's similar to those of a demagogue who claims that his views are the truth and all other views are "ideology." Human culture is made up of contending ideologies, and Saul's "humanism" is merely one of them. Civilization depends upon the ability of humanity to recognize, through self-reflection and examination, the unconscious ideological convictions that cause people to hold beliefs and the relativity of those beliefs. The fact that I agree with many of Saul's particular ideological positions—that church and state should be separate; that multiracial, multiethnic, and multicultural societies are preferable to artificially "pure" ones; and that compromise and conciliation are preferable to absolutism and oppression—does not oblige me to repeat the absolutist fallacy of claiming to have no ideology.

Saul's discussion in his "Humanism" entry is similarly troublesome. His definition comes at the end of the entry: "We fail ourselves. But if we know that, then we can also find ways to save ourselves. That is the essence of humanism" (168). Indeed, the notion that as human beings we are alone in the world and responsible for our own success or failure, and that our various ethical, aesthetic, and material successes reflect not fate, or divine intervention, or the processes of nature, but our own innate, free, conscious, and indomitable qualities, is fundamental to humanism. However, it is not a notion widely shared by African or Asian or Amerindian cultures.

The major difficulty with such absolutist ideological positions as the one implicit in Saul's definition of humanism is that they are based on the assumption that there are eternal, transcendent, unchanging concepts or entities—the Judaeo-Christian and Muslim "God," Plato's "the Good," the Franco-American concept of "Liberty," which led presidential candidate Barry Goldwater to make the muddled observation, "Extremism in the defence of liberty is no vice." At the basis of humanism and its "essence" is the concept of the eternal "spirit of man," which Renaissance thinkers attempted to place at the centre of creation, and which Victorian thinkers attempted to substitute for "God" as Western society became increasingly sceptical and secular. Midway through his definition, Saul approvingly cites fifteenth-century philosopher and scholar Pico della Mirandola, "who in his *Oration on the Dignity of Man* has God tell Adam, 'I have placed you at the centre of the world so that from there you may see what is in it.'"

This assertion, that mankind is positioned at the centre of creation, is, of course, an ideological one, and in the history of Western thought it is notable as part of a general shift from earlier medieval ideologies. Saul seems aware of humanism's relative place within human culture when he remarks, "These simple notions are central to the Western idea of civilization," and he is apparently acknowledging that there could be, outside the West, other ideas of civilization. But he immediately follows this with another assertion that humanism is not an ideology: the "simple notions" are "clearly opposed to the narrow and mechanistic certainties of ideology" (165). Again, this seems like intellectual chicanery, another example of Saul's habit of asserting, "What *you* believe is mere ideology, but what we in the West believe, or what we humanists believe, is the truth." Saul misuses the word *ideology* hundreds of times in this book and in subsequent ones, as if by doing so he will normalize the misuse and render his readers unconscious of his deception.

Saul's *The Unconscious Civilization* repeats in overtly simplified form the arguments of the two preceding works, suggesting in its title and opening chapters that contemporary culture has become irresponsibly oblivious to, or "unconscious" of, its acquiescence to managerialism. Once again, Saul pretends not to know that the main characteristic of ideology is that it is "unconscious," and that he too, like all human beings, has unconscious beliefs and attitudes that require a continuous process of self-examination to bring even to partial consciousness. He also pretends not to know that if there is blame to be assigned, it's not for *having* unconscious views—since we all have them—but for being, like Saul himself, unwilling to admit that we have them and are influenced by them. Here his argument reduces to, "What you believe is unconscious, but what I believe and write is conscious and therefore credible."

The fact that this book, the slightest of Saul's nonfiction, won three major Canadian literary awards, including the Governor General's Award for nonfiction, while the two larger books won little, says much about the intellectual level of Canada's literary jurors and their capacity to reward persistence and celebrity. Saul's *Doubter's Companion* definition of "Awards Show" may be, in this case, appropriate: "Mechanism by which the members of a given profession attempt to give themselves the attributes of the pre-modern ruling classes—the military, aristocracy and priest-hood—by assigning various orders, decorations, and medals to each other" (33). It is arguably appropriate also to the numerous Order of Canada awards shows that Saul, as Mr. G.G., now has to witness.

Reflections of a Siamese Twin: Canada at the End of the Twentieth Century offers somewhat more than Fetherling suggests in his understandably cynical characterization of it: "Saul revisiting the basic ideas of the earlier works in order to apply them to Canada." Saul indeed repeats his claims about the cultural domination of managers and systems analysts, and he argues that contemporary Canadian politicians such as Mike Harris and Bernard Landry exemplify the type. But he also rehearses much of the central-Canadian cultural analysis of Harold Innis, George Grant, Northrop Frye, Marshall McLuhan, and Margaret Atwood, blurring their often conflicting ideas into his own theory of a historically cooperative, landscape-respecting, communications-based, and compromise-creating culture that built an experimental, nonrational country, despite being surrounded by the values of Voltaire's bastards. The power of this book resides not only in its offering of an idealized Canada, the country of Clarkson's "decent" and "generous" people—one in which many Canadian readers would like to see themselves "reflected"—but also in its implicit offering of the gallant Canada of Clarkson's installation speech. That Canada, at least until the emergence of Reaganite technocrats like Harris and Landry, in Saul's view, often quietly defied the dominant managerialism of other countries.

Here, again, Saul's repeated idiosyncratic use of the word *ideology* is a leitmotif. His use of *elites* is equally repetitive. In *Voltaire* and *Doubters*, he often employs the term to refer to those who enjoy political or economic power, who perform technocratic or bureaucratic tasks, or who do not share his views on economic, military, and political history. In the word, a reader can detect echoes of Saul's descriptions of his doctoral examiners and of the sceptical reviewers of his books. Saul's elites are educated, but not necessarily in humanistic studies, they are generally not trustworthy, they are interested in maintaining their social and economic advantages over others, they define success and pleasure in terms of material gain. Specifically, in *Reflections* they are "those in positions of responsibility," they are Canada's "colonial-minded leadership," they are "politicians, creative people, businessmen" (16, 69). They are colonial because they are overly impressed with how things are done in the United States, Britain, or France, because they prefer the culture of those countries, and because they rank the approval of the powerful in such countries above the well-being of their fellow citizens.

Saul's description could include numerous Canadian artists and writers who have sought international awards or spent substantial parts of their careers living in Paris, London, or New York: "people who have a talent for appreciating the brilliance of what is done elsewhere" (470). It could include writers Callaghan, Ondaatje, Gallant, Richler, Atwood, and Levine, dramatist Robert Lepage, painters Jack Bush and Attila Lukacs. It could include Clarkson and Saul. However, Saul usually steers his condemnation towards multinational businessmen and right-of-centre political leaders who have supported free trade or the Meech Lake Accord or attempted to "open Canada up for business."

Saul's message throughout *Reflections* is that he is wary of Canada's "elites," and that ordinary nonelite Canadians should be wary of them also. This is a populist message, delivered in a loose, colloquial style designed to disguise the fact that the author holds a PhD (a fact not mentioned in the dust-jacket copy—although, ironically, it does include the statement, "Saul was recently named a chevalier of the prestigious French Ordre des Arts et des Lettres")—and to create the illusion that he is just another ordinary Canadian. It is directed to the nonelite, warning them that they and their jobs and their nation risk being sold out by "anti-democratic elites," a "large panoply of those with responsibility, from ministers to intellectuals to businessmen," who are willing to advance themselves within global "corporatist" culture by betraying their nation (253, 266). They do this, in part, Saul claims, because they have acquiesced, like Brian Mulroney (one of Saul's most frequent targets), to the colonial idea that the globalization of manufacturing, finance, trade, and culture is inevitable. While Saul's general critique here of globalization and its supporters is persuasive, his Manichean division of Canadians into ordinary democrats and antidemocratic elites is invidious. In reality, many Canadian doctors, teachers, labour leaders, "intellectuals," civil servants, politicians, and federal cabinet ministers have serious reservations about technocratic economic and cultural globalization and have refused to accept that it is inevitable. In 1988, numerous members of the intellectual "elite" published statements opposing free trade. Many Canadians have mixed feelings about the issue—a position that Saul usually tries to ignore—and they have hoped that a democratization of globalization will allow the continuation of democratic local and national decision making.

On Equilibrium is Saul's attempt to articulate an alternative to managerialism, partly in terms of the balances and compromises he describes Canadians as having achieved historically in *Reflections*. Here, one of Saul's examples of managerialism is

President George W. Bush, who has attempted to "manage" international terrorism by avoiding compromise and nuanced thinking, and by reducing the concept of terrorism to a simple "us" versus "them." It was Saul's having appeared to insult Bush through this argument while occupying the residence of Canada's symbolic head of state that gave the book much of its initial publicity. However, the book's main emphasis falls on six of what Saul calls "qualities": common sense, ethics, imagination, intuition, memory, and reason. He argues that these are essential to human beings and that, if used "consciously" (a reference to his *The Unconscious Civilization*) and "in balance" with one another, they can help achieve "equilibrium."

Exactly why these are "qualities" rather than "aspects" or "abilities" of human beings, Saul does not explain. They are clearly not parallel concepts: *imagination* and *intuition* are overlapping terms, as are *intuition* and *common sense*; *ethics* is usually considered to be a field of inquiry or a set of principles rather than a human attribute. Furthermore, Saul does not explain why these particular qualities are more important than others, or whether the six form an exhaustive list. Presumably, *courage* could be on such a list, or *integrity*. Moreover, Saul's six terms themselves have a history of conflicting usage. His understanding of *common sense,* for example, differs from the British cultural studies understanding of the term as denoting false knowledge that is popularly taken for granted as true. It differs, as well, from Mike Harris's understanding of it as denoting desirably systematic managerial practices—an understanding that Harris encapsulated in his 1995 political slogan "the Common Sense Revolution."

On Equilibrium is a loosely conceived and subjective book of cracker-barrel philosophy, which paradoxically invokes many of the leading names of formal philosophy. It is not all that dissimilar from various psychological self-help books that promise the reader a sense of well-being. The book also appears to be Saul's attempt to reduce the antagonistic structures—unconscious versus conscious, reason versus imagination, managerialism versus humanism, managers versus visionaries—that permeated his previous works. His concept of equilibrium questions the historic Western emphasis on conquest, expansion, and domination, and it stands as a metaphor for cultural coexistence, ecological conservation, and a steady, nonexpansionist economy. While these are arguably general philosophical matters, they are also matters that play various roles in the positions of Canadian political parties, and they underlie current disputes among Canada and other nation-states—on the Kyoto Accord on greenhouse gas emissions, for example, or on development of Alaska's Northern Slope oil fields—and so they are arguably also political. Much of Saul's argument here is supported, as it is in his other books, by selective evidence, fragmentary quotation, persuasively narrated but unproven anecdote, and enormous generalizations such as the assertion that it was "the Christian civilization and no other which massacred six million Jews." This is about as socially and academically useful as the old Christian assertion that "the Jews killed Christ."

Nevertheless, *On Equilibrium* is essentially a good-news book. It holds that individuals have access to the means of balancing their lives within an unbalanced Western culture. It parallels the "good news" of Adrienne Clarkson's many speeches: that it is "wonderful" to be here, that Canada has a "northern" history of social caring, that Canadians are "decent" people who have willingly balanced and compromised to achieve "triangular" goodwill among anglophone, francophone, aboriginal, and other culturally distinct Canadians. These are not great, geometrically persuasive, or necessarily true ideas, but they have their political function.

In his official role as "His Excellency," Saul has given many fewer speeches than Clarkson, although, surprisingly, they have been much more political. Like his books, his speeches are badly organized. They are held together by repeated summaries and phrases such as (all from the same speech): "I keep saying," "What I'm saying is," "Let me finish," "What have I said so far," "I'd like to finish," "What am I saying" (archived speech, 18 May 2000). In his speeches, Saul repeats many of the statements and themes from his books, including those that Clarkson has taken as her own. "Half a century ago, we murdered seven million Jews," he told the International Council for Canadian Studies in May of 2000, presumably speaking not merely as a Canadian or secret Nazi or junior governor general, but as a member of "Christian civilization." Canada is "a poor northern society," he informed the same audience, "which has intellectually constructed its prosperity through an idea of inclusive egalitarianism," thereby developing the joint Saul/Clarkson theme that northern countries are naturally inclined to collective social action. In 133 years of history, he insisted, repeating his argument that Canadians have a historic attraction to compromise, only "about 85" Canadians have "died as a result of civil strife." Canada is "an old civilization," he told the same audience in May 2000; in November 1999, he had told a British Columbia audience that this is "an old country" that long ago "put together aboriginals, francophones and anglophones" (archived speeches, 18 May 2000, 19 Nov. 1999).

A recurrent theme in Saul's speeches is that because Canadians did things a certain way in the past, they should do them similarly in the future. He repeatedly refers to the close relationship between Robert Baldwin and Louis Lafontaine—the focus of his annual Baldwin-Lafontaine Symposium—and, as he does in *Reflections*, he urges that it should be a model for contemporary cultural cooperation. In a convocation address he delivered at Simon Fraser University, Saul promoted a return to universal public education because it is "our past, our foundations" (archived speech, 5 Oct. 2000). He also referred to his idea of a "triangular foundation" and implied that this foundation is now becoming contemporary policy: "Slowly but surely we've been re-remembering that original triangular foundation" (archived speech, 18 May 2000). The argument that foundational practice is necessarily good is a strange one, given that nations have historically made mistakes—like the nation that participated in the murder of "seven million Jews."

Saul is also insistent that social action be accomplished through democratic process. On three occasions, he has declared himself adamantly opposed to charity, an opposition more gently expressed by Clarkson in her speech to the Canadian Association of Foodbanks on June 1, 2001. In his March 2000 inauguration speech at the Baldwin-Lafontaine Symposium, he criticized charity for being an antidemocratic approach because it allows "those *with*" to "get to choose who and how to help those *without*." He declared that Strindberg was right in saying, "All charity is humiliating." He went on to criticize the replacement of "universal" public programs (presumably programs like family allowance or the old-age pension) with "targeted public programs." This, he said, took us back to "plain old charity," "back to the old top down, judgmental and eventually moralizing approach to those who have problems" (archived speech, 23 Mar. 2000).

In his Simon Fraser convocation address, Saul urged public

funding of university education and condemned reliance on scholarships, because they "mean that we require those with less to be smarter than those with more in order to get an equal chance." He continued: "People talk of bursaries. What is this desire of those in authority to count the income of those with less and then to judge how much they deserve? This is classic noblesse oblige. Strindberg said 'All charity is humiliating.' That is why an egalitarian society such as ours has been built upon universal, inclusive principles, public education first among them."

In a speech to the Forum on Volunteerism, he proclaimed that "charity isn't supposed to be a necessary requirement of the functioning of a democratic society," and he again quoted Strindberg—this time as having said, "All charity is humiliation" (archived speech, 18 Aug. 2000). At the time Saul gave these speeches, many conservative provincial governments, ideologically committed to the principle that individuals are responsible for looking after their own lives, including finding money for food and education, were increasing university tuition fees, cutting back on housing allowances to people on welfare, and searching for "welfare cheats." The federal government had eliminated universal payment of child allowances, converting it to a tax credit for low-income workers, and it had begun clawing back a portion of the old-age pension by making its benefits taxable. These issues have been the subject of intense political dispute, and Saul was using his position as Mr. G.G. to intervene. And while I agree strongly with his arguments about charity, I would be extremely unhappy if another governor-general's spouse were to use his or her unearned patronage position to publicize and promote regressive social policy. On the basis of Saul's own arguments, to use his position to advance any political cause is undemocratic.

In his Baldwin-Lafontaine lecture, Saul opposed NGOs (non-governmental international lobby groups such as Greenpeace or the nationalist Council of Canadians) on grounds similar to those on which he opposed charity and selective social programs—that they are undemocratic. He argued that NGOs, which he defined as "corporation[s] of social reformers," have the structure and employ the practices of commercial corporations, and, like such corporations, they are answerable not to the general public but to their own members. They perform the work previously done by democratic process but do not "feed into it." "In a curious way," he said, "the very success of those NGOs most devoted to the public good actually undermines the democratic process—the actual guarantor of the public good—because they don't feed into it."

Two weeks earlier, he had made a related argument about globalization and the nation-state, arguing that the nation-state is the only entity in which a citizen can currently be represented, and that on democratic grounds, the nation-state needs to be strengthened, not transcended or discarded. This strengthening would not be "a return to the state but rather . . . a return to the citizenry," and it should lead to global agreements that are in the interest of citizens rather than multinational corporations— "agreements on the social aspects of things, on working conditions, on taxes, on culture" (archived speech, 9 Mar. 2001).

Both Clarkson and Saul have been perceived as extreme left-of-centre activists by many media commentators. Yet there is very little evidence in their writing and speeches to support such a characterization. Despite moments of socialism in their thoughts about charity, the Canadian political philosophy to which they are closest is Red Toryism. This philosophy envisions a diverse but harmonious state that protects the weak and encourages the creative. It remembers and idealizes—as in the writings of George Grant—past ages of social cooperation in which workers enjoyed "organic" relationships to their work, golden ages that never existed in quite such an idealized form. Clarkson and Saul do not imagine a radical new future, nor do they propose ways of being or governing that are unprecedented. They repeatedly call on Canadians to return to older, "foundational" ways of doing things—to the model of Athenian democracy, to the social caring of the Dene and the Inuit, to "the Canadian tradition," to the Canadian constitutional thought of Baldwin and Lafontaine, to the ideals of public education of the late nineteenth century, to the allegedly "triangular" ethnic thinking of Canada's founders. Saul, particularly, calls Canadians away from newer institutions and concepts such as multinational corporations, NGOs, and consumerism. He calls them away from the concept of continuous economic growth and back to democracy, citizenship, humanism, public education, and a pre-Industrial Revolution economics of equilibrium, because these things are "our past, our foundations."

Either one of the G.G.s would have been a strong successor to Joe Clark as Progressive Conservative leader, if only because both are intuitive believers in bedrock Tory ideology. Clarkson could have been an extremely successful replacement for Clark—one needs only to imagine how her installation speech would have been received as a leadership victory speech. "Embark on a journey with me" would have been a message at least as powerful as any heard by Canadians from Tory leaders since the "northern vision" of John Diefenbaker. The time will come when she'll be prime minister, Clarkson's colleague Allan Fotheringham has predicted on at least two occasions (1985, 1986). She may have sold herself and history short by agreeing to be only Mrs. G.G.

Sophisticated Adrienne

OR: I'm Very Hedonistic
Weeping for Fred Astaire

Today I thought of going out and buying a bottle of wine to celebrate my completion of Take Six. I looked at the liquor board's latest Vintages catalogue. Here was an article about John Ralston Saul and the cellar of Canadian wine he has assembled at Rideau Hall. "We are the great northern nation," Saul was telling the liquor board's David Churchill. "We produce a northern style of food and we produce a northern style of wines"—presumably to drink while practising a "northern style" of social responsibility. All the other themes of his books and Clarkson's speeches were also packed into Saul's comments to Churchill; here, however, he wasn't applying them to caring Canadians but to the complexity of wine. "At Rideau Hall," Saul declared, as if he were delivering or writing yet another viceregal speech, which I suppose in a sense he was, "we serve teas, such as (a very refreshing) Cloudberry, made by the Inuit in Arpiqutik, Northern Quebec. We are at the base an Anglo/Franco/Aboriginal society. We are also a very old culture, contrary to popular belief. We are one of the most open and welcoming societies in the world. We are a country of high consciousness, self-control, and a greater layer of complexity than we give ourselves credit for."

And thus we make complex teas and wines and produce a "sophisticated" governor general. One more pass through my clippings.

I love anything designed by Giorgio Armani. (Clarkson, quoted in Gould)

What my humanist education did for me was summed up beautifully by Northrop Frye in one of his essays. It helped make me sophisticated. (Clarkson, archived speech, 13 Nov. 2001)

When thus declaring herself "sophisticated," Clarkson was speaking at McGill University's fall convocation. At first one wonders if she was being ironic or self-mocking. But no, she continues with a solemn Northrop Frye quotation and more serious pronouncements: "'Sophistication,' says Frye, is simply 'the ability to encounter culture with the minimum amount of anxiety.' And in encountering culture, one develops an understanding that the criterion of all culture is excellence. Excellence is the only thing that matters in the final product of the artistic vision and in the scholarly search for truth."

Perhaps the initial thing to note in this passage is Clarkson's very specific use of the word *culture*. She is not using it in the general sociological sense in which one speaks of "Canadian culture." Nor is she using it in the anthropological sense in which "culture" is distinguished from "nature," and in which there can be "Stone Age cultures" or "mass culture." As her statement "the criterion of all culture is excellence" reveals, she is using it as a synonym for "high culture" in the Matthew Arnold tradition of speaking of "culture" as something more refined and civilized than "barbarism," "philistinism," or "materialism" (all of which, of course, are in an anthropological sense cultural expressions). So, when she declares herself "sophisticated," she is declaring that, in the colloquial sense of the word, she is "cultured" and therefore an "Excellency" who is possessed of "excellence."

The second thing to note is that Clarkson narrows Frye's observation about anxiety to that caused by class difference, even though anxiety or insecurity can be caused by almost any cultural difference. I, for example, may experience anxiety upon entering a Hindu temple in Bangalore because I know that I am unaware of local religious customs. But Clarkson's anxiety is extremely specific. It is the anxiety of the country person who is invited to the urban and urbane mansion that houses "excellent" objects and "excellent" ideas—the products "of artistic vision and . . . the scholarly search for truth." It is the anxiety of the person who wishes to be found acceptable by those who are "cultured."

Sophistication, of course, is not the only attribute that helps one avoid such anxiety. Ignorance would suffice, if it included ignorance of the possibility that the other's culture might be more "excellent" than one's own. Disdain might also serve, if one had reason to believe that the other's claims to "excellence" were simply vanity and pretension. Scepticism—or what Saul calls "doubt" in his *Doubter's Companion*—could work very well, especially since "excellence" is so vaguely defined by Clarkson, much the way "the best" is vaguely defined by Arnold. As Pierre Bourdieu has observed in *The Rules of Art,* concepts like "excellence" and "best" usually just describe the current preferences of those who possess cultural power and influence.

In another speech, this one to guests at a reception held at the Shakespeare Festival in Stratford, Ontario—a Canadian site of high culture if there ever was one—Clarkson related one of her key moments of such anxiety. It occurred in 1951, when she was in her early teens and living in Ottawa. She had convinced her parents to allow her to go to the opening season of the Stratford festival. "I remember it as a defining moment of my life," she began. "First of all, it was the first time I took the train by myself from Ottawa to Toronto, and my mother lent me her jade pin to wear with my grey suit. And then I was met very royally at the train station by Mr. and Mrs. Vanderploeg. We went right away to dinner at the Royal York Hotel in the Imperial Room and had roast beef and then I stayed at their house in the Kingsway, which was wonderful and filled with copies of *The New Yorker*. And it was the first time I'd ever seen *The New Yorker* magazine and its cartoons. And I knew, without being told, what sophistication meant" (archived speech, 25 Sept. 2001).

The unsophisticated child sets out hopefully. She is wearing her grey suit, to fit in and claim respectability, and her mother's jade pin, to make a small ethnic claim to good taste and elegance. Arriving in Toronto, she is greeted—"met very *royally*"—with a deluge of signs of upper-class taste. She is taken to the *Royal* York Hotel, to the *Imperial* Room, and to a house on the *King*sway. She is fed roast beef, the symbolic meal of the anglo establishment, and then she encounters something newer and even more glamorous than the Royal *York*: *The New Yorker*. Again, the reader wonders for a moment whether Clarkson is being ironic in equating the cliquish liberal New York City magazine with "sophistication" and mocking her naive teenage self. But no, she continues to describe that self as being "transported" by what she encountered, as being "really hooked," and thereafter travelling to Stratford "almost every season." In light of Clarkson's having become, forty-seven years later, the royal surrogate, the Canadian stand-in for the sophisticated queen herself, the anecdote reads like the beginning of a Cinderella story: the peasant girl discovers the royal realm and realizes that she may belong there herself, despite her humble, "grey suit" origins.

In both these Clarkson passages, there is a sense of naivety that belies the claim to sophistication. In the first, she seems unaware that to claim sophistication is not a sophisticated thing to do, and that it can easily be read as an anxiety signal. She also seems gloriously unaware that the term *excellence*, and similar idealist superlatives loved by Matthew Arnold, have long been empty words in our language. They've been confined to the world of advertising, where universities and automobile manufactures alike claim them; they are empty words that do little except activate people's fraud detectors. In the second passage, she seems unaware that the Royal York Hotel stands in Canadian culture as a symbol of central Canadian wealth and privilege—of uncaring wealth, in the novels of Morley Callaghan—and that to many Torontonians a Kingsway address signifies the blandness of the old-time bourgeoisie.

Even her choice of the word *sophistication* seems somewhat naive, particularly given her training in English literature. The word descends from the medieval *sophistic*—which meant "characterised by specious reasoning." The verb *sophisticate* came to mean "to adulterate," or "to corrupt," or "to render less genuine or honest." The *Oxford English Dictionary*, from which I take these definitions, gives assorted meanings for *sophisticated*. Its first definition is, "Mixed with some foreign substance; adulterated; not pure or genuine." Its second has three parts: the first, "Altered from, or deprived of, primitive simplicity or naturalness"; the second, "Of a person: free of naivete, experienced, worldly-wise; subtle, discriminating, refined, cultured"; the third, "Of equipment, techniques, theories, etc.: employing advanced or refined methods or concepts; highly developed or complicated." Its third definition is in two parts: the first, "Falsified in a greater or lesser degree; not plain, honest, or straightforward"; the second, "Of a printed book, containing alterations in content, binding, etc., which are intended to deceive." In contemporary usage, the understanding of the word as a synonym for "worldly" or "intellectually advanced" is widely associated with connotations of superficiality, fraudulence, pretension, and life in the fast lane—with upper-class taste, expensive wines, expensive holidays and cars. One example is found in this CNN Interactive headline: New York designer Bill "Blass Brings Hallmark Sophistication to Fall Fashion" (7 Sept. 1966). Another is in this headline from the *Detroit Free Press*: "Sophistication Rules at Uber-Cool Lounge" (6 July 2001).

Such mixed understandings of Clarkson and her "sophistication" have been prominently expressed during all phases of her career, most often in terms of her taste in home decorating. Commentators have posed various binary questions: Is Clarkson sophisticated or merely narcissistic? Is she sophisticated or merely hedonistic? Do the heavily adorned surfaces of her body and her homes display her taste or merely her overflowing self-indulgence? In her 1969 *Chatelaine* profile of Clarkson, Catherine Breslin was one of the first to make such an inquiry. In the profile's early pages, Breslin adopts a friendly and nonjudgemental tone, especially when she focuses on Clarkson's *Take 30* experience, her background, and her childhood. But as soon as Breslin enters Clarkson's Rosedale home, her tone starts to display an intermittent critical edge, and she presents Clarkson's sophistication as excessive and self-indulgent: "At home, she and Stephen may dine alone or throw a dinner party for eight. In either case, they serve themselves from silver platters and eat with sterling forks. A few nights a week they go out to meetings. Otherwise, they sit in their study, classical music sifting from the phonograph."

The implication of unseemly luxury is abrupt. The Clarksons have not one but numerous "silver platters"; they don't save the "good" silver for their guests but use it themselves for casual dining; they frequently and impulsively "throw a dinner party for eight." Juxtaposed with the silver platters and the sterling forks, the "sifting" of the "classical music"—which might otherwise have seemed unexceptional—signals false upper-class sophistication.

Breslin then gazes around Clarkson's home and initiates the journalistic tradition of interpreting and judging Clarkson through her taste in furnishings and clothing. "If she doesn't look like the Canadian girl next door," Breslin begins, "that's because she isn't . . . Her house is furnished in an exotic blend of French inlaid antiques, English tapestry chairs, Russian icons, Chinese jade figurines, Canadian oil paintings and a couple of thousand books. Presiding over it is 'The Woman,' a seven-foot $1,800 modern wood sculpture of a pregnant lady that Adrienne gave to Steve for his birthday . . . Her clothes are divided between exquisitely made French originals, bought on a once-a-year shopping spree in Paris, and splashy little things from Toronto boutiques."

Breslin's remark that Clarkson is not "like the Canadian girl next door" suggests that this woman is removed from Canadian-ness by her "exotic," expensive, possibly profligate, international tastes. Curiously, Breslin even implies that possessing "a couple of thousand books" is as non-Canadian as possessing Russian icons and French inlaid antiques. Breslin's reference to the wood sculpture and her juxtaposition of Clarkson's home decoration and clothing specifically gender the home and blur any division between it and a woman's body. Home and body are similarly and excessively decorated, and they become interchangeable. Clarkson's body—which is pregnant with her first child—seems for Breslin to spill its sophisticated excesses into the home, into its "exotic blend" of adornments, its statue of the pregnant woman. The home becomes Clarkson, and Clarkson's exotic, well-decorated, and cosmopolitan body becomes indistinguishable from the home.

However, Breslin returns to a nonjudgemental tone for a few more paragraphs until, just before the end of the article, she asks Clarkson about her plans for the future. The answers Clarkson provides seem ordinary: "She's asked about getting into the control booth to learn production; as a confirmed movie buff she might write a film script, or learn to direct. She certainly expects to write more books." But then Clarkson offers her interviewer an irresistible quote: "'I'm very hedonistic,' she smiles. 'I enjoy doing what I want and being what I want. We're absolutely believers in Live Now.'"

Clarkson's naive and enthusiastic display of narcissism quickly returns Breslin to the theme that Canada is too small for Clarkson as well as to the theme of the excess implicit in Clarkson's clothing and home decoration. "Steve has been considering going to teach at the University of Tanzania in Dar-es-Salaam for a year or two," Clarkson confides, and the "year or two" underlines how luxuriously casual and unpressured such choices are for her husband. In her concluding paragraph, Breslin reveals that Clarkson wants to "see Tahiti and the Inca ruins of Peru. Visit Hunza, a dot of geography north of Nepal. 'It's Shangri-La, and I'd adore to see the Himalayas.' She'd like to take a boat cruise around the world for a year, 'very slow and comfortable.'"

Here—"I'd adore to see the Himalayas"—is the climax of the article and the pinnacle of Clarkson's ambitions, all of them exotic, self-indulgent, frivolously conceived. Clarkson appears to show no interest in the people or social problems of these places; she's only concerned about her own "slow and comfortable" pleasure. And her greatest ambition, Breslin announces in concluding, is to dance with Fred Astaire: "I watch his old movies on TV," she quotes Clarkson, "and I *cry*."

It is not clear whether Breslin set out to do a hatchet job on Clarkson. The profile's early pages suggest that she didn't. But the more Breslin sees of Clarkson's private life, her domestic spaces, and her private ambitions, the more angrily lower class Breslin herself seems to feel, and the more damaging to Clarkson become the small details that Breslin reveals and the juxtapositions and emphases that she creates. The profile's final paragraph, in which Breslin depicts Clarkson as fascinated with her own emotional responses—adoring the Himalayas, crying over the grace of Fred Astaire—adroitly creates a figure who seems committed to banal pleasures and self-trivialization. Again, her "sophistication" seems to spill over, but now as emotionality and tears.

Three years later, journalist Melinda McCracken undertook a

similar profile for *Maclean's* and, like Breslin, she visited Adrienne and Stephen Clarkson's Rosedale home. Clearly, from the beginning, there was an enormous class chasm between McCracken and the expensive and elegantly constructed domestic space she had entered—a chasm that McCracken herself acknowledged by describing her own faded jeans, uncut hair, lack of makeup, and girlish voice.

After being ushered into the living room by Professor Clarkson, McCracken looks around and sees, "Broadloom, Victorian settee, sofa and two matching chairs, the oil painting with the small birdlike shape emerging from an off-centre point, Borduas over the mantle, velvet curtains. Everything has a sense of having been carefully considered, of meeting certain personal requirements. The things are beautiful, interesting in themselves, in proportion with each other, historically and personally significant. It is an intensely cultural room; the actual value of the objects appears to be relatively unimportant."

It may seem a little strange that McCracken is impressed by broadloom, which Canadian working-class families began ordering from the Eaton's and Simpsons-Sears catalogues in the 1950s. Nonetheless, McCracken is culturally astute enough to identify and be impressed by many of the special, limited-availability elements of the room: the Victorian settee, the painting by Paul-Émile Borduas. But what especially impresses and amazes her is not that a person of about her own age can possess these objects, but that such a person is free to pick and choose from among similar items, to "carefully consider" and select elements that meet her "personal requirements" while remaining "in proportion to each other." In fact, Clarkson's ability to design and construct an integrated array of possessions without having to consider their cost or "value" astonishes McCracken so much that she lingers over the matter for several more sentences: "Everything relates subtly to everything else in colour—rose, gold, and olive green—and in form, but not in period or national origin . . . Nothing jars, it all blends into a harmonious traditional whole, touched by the same mind."

Like Breslin, McCracken later sees a resemblance between this scene of intense design and Clarkson's personal image, which, she suggests, "has all the approved symbols: MAs, PhDs, the right schools (St. Hilda's at Trinity), the right class (upper middle), the right clothes (Paris originals, until haute couture fell), the right house in the right place (modified establishment), the right sorts of involvements, associations with the right sorts of people . . ."

Again, she juxtaposes Clarkson's clothing and house, subtly suggesting that she dresses both, and that her body extends symbolically through the house to her "involvements" and "associations." While there may be some envy in the particulars of her list of "symbols," McCracken's main perception is the astonished one she had earlier—"It all looks like it might have happened naturally as much as by design." That is, the array of elements that constitute Clarkson's image only "looks like" it didn't happen by design. To McCracken, creating the *illusion* of accidental elegance is the utmost contrivance, and she eventually admits that this is the conclusion she has reached about Clarkson's domain: "to me it's all contrived, a total fabrication." She then asks, "What drives a person to do everything in her power to become someone else?"

Of course, in some ways we all contrive our own images, including McCracken. She has contrived her own appearance of naturalness and simplicity—declining to wear makeup or cut her hair, wearing faded jeans to a Rosedale visit. The revelation that Clarkson's image or domestic space could be contrived is not of significance here; it is the elements she has used in the contrivance that are worth noting, and the fact that her desired image is cultured and tasteful. Clarkson, for her part, appears to have received McCracken with politeness, civility, and, at times (perhaps she was remembering Breslin's visit), understandable caution. She even briefly confided in McCracken some thoughts about her recent "melancholy." This was one of the most intimate moments any interviewer has ever shared with Clarkson. McCracken, perhaps distracted by the harmonious decor, appears not to have noticed what her interview was achieving. Also, she doesn't seem to have noticed the condescension in Clarkson's comment that sometimes she has failed at things because she has "accepted a lesser person's judgement," with its implication that Clarkson herself is a "greater person."

Urjo Kareda interviewed Clarkson fourteen years later, in Paris, while she was serving as Ontario's agent general. Like McCracken's, Kareda's article begins with a strong emphasis on decor, elegance, and self-construction. His metaphor for the latter—befitting his career as a theatre critic—is theatrical performance, rather than McCracken's static metaphor of "image." Again, there is a marked gendering of Clarkson's space as female and an implication that her body extends itself into her surroundings. Kareda sees folds of cloth everywhere, on Clarkson herself and on the walls of her home: she and they are "dressed." "The fabric of Adrienne Clarkson's world has a luxurious texture," he begins, "the shimmering extravagance of silk or the subtle elegance of cashmere falling naturally into sculpted drapery. She dresses with a flawless sense of drama." Here Kareda creates the same paradox that McCracken did between the seemingly natural and the contrived—the cashmere that falls "naturally" into "sculpted" drapery. He returns to this paradox when describing Clarkson's personality: "Above all, the personality is commanding, weaving together charm and authority, spontaneity and control, modesty and arrogance. Her presentation of herself defies you not to admire. Adrienne Clarkson is a consummate performer in the theatre of herself." Like McCracken, Kareda is immediately attracted by the decor of the rooms, believing that Clarkson herself has determined how they will be painted and furnished. Both interviewers are also impressed by their subject's fashionable address. For Ontario's offices, Clarkson has chosen the Faubourg, which is, at the very least, the Rosedale of Paris.

Two years before Kareda, Sheila Ward was also impressed by the address and had quickly associated Clarkson with high fashion, expensive taste, and old European elegance. "La rue du Faubourg St. Honoré," she had begun an otherwise uninteresting article and interview for the *Metropolitan Toronto Business Journal,* "winds its way through the fashionable and expensive eighth district in Paris, its cobblestone road and narrow sidewalks passing the doors of the great fashion houses of Cardin, Feraud, and Lanvin, among others." But Kareda's eyes take us inside as well. "Her office on the rue du Faubourg Saint-Honoré insists on its occupant's style," he tells us. "Few government offices are designed to complement an official's colour scheme, but in Clarkson's office—with its shadings from pale mauve to deepest purple—one feels that nothing she wears will ever clash with the wall. The office suggests both femininity and power, as well as the taste of the woman it displays." It is as if, for Kareda, even the wall has become a fashion accessory to the clothes Clarkson wears. And while McCracken merely sees in the Rosedale rooms an attempt to display upper-middle-class casual good taste, Kareda sees something even more ambitious, personally assertive, and imperial. "It is a contemporary democrat's memory of an empress's throne room, and Adrienne Clarkson looks at home in it."

Kareda is similarly surprised when he gets to visit Clarkson and Saul's "large and elegant" apartment, located in another fashionable area of central Paris, Les Invalides: "Guests drift though the huge, superbly appointed living room, flawless with its dark, stately colours, its magnificent fresh flowers, its Canadian paintings and Oriental artefacts, its artwork furniture." The words he uses to describe the room seem unconsciously to evoke Clarkson: "dark," "superb," "flawless," "stately," "magnificent," "Canadian," "Oriental," and "artwork." One wonders whether McCracken would have been able to survive such intensely personal opulence. Kareda, however, keeps in mind that this apartment is not only Clarkson and Saul's home but also a working space. On one night during his visit, Clarkson entertains forty French journalists, and on another she hosts a performance by pianist Angela Hewitt and a screening of a CBC film on Glenn Gould. He sees that Clarkson treats the apartment as a set for the exuberant playacting she must do on such occasions. Nevertheless, his brief description of the apartment, and of Clarkson creating "the illusion of friendship" for her guests, again suggests the strength and overflowing extravagance of her talent for artifice. Kareda also depicts Clarkson and Saul entertaining visitors in a study while sitting under a large oil portrait of themselves—a sly hint of royal narcissism.

If, over the years, few journalists seem to have been afforded a glimpse of Clarkson's domestic rooms, it may be due to Breslin, McCracken, and Kareda. All three used what they saw to create at times unflattering portrayals of their subject. McCracken's article, according to the *Toronto Star*'s Philip Marchand, was a "notorious" prank perpetrated on Clarkson by *Maclean's* editors Peter Newman and Don Obe: "take a radical in faded jeans and red bandanna around her neck (McCracken), put her in Clarkson's living room, and watch the fur fly." Kareda's more balanced and good-humoured article subtly mocked Clarkson's empress-like pretensions ("her regal office") and the slightness of her television accomplishments ("a journalist who by interviewing celebrities became a celebrity herself").

The only other journalist to testify about the Clarkson-Saul living quarters is John Lownsbrough. The quarters he visited, sometime in 1994, was their Toronto townhouse, which, a year later, would be feminized by Val Ross to become a "jewelbox townhouse." Lownsbrough was admitted to the home not by Clarkson, but by Saul. His article begins with a description of the place, but first he comments on the couple's "lofty aesthetic standards, standards neither of them is exactly demure about enunciating or defending." This comment places Lownsbrough's description into a context of dubious aesthetics ("lofty" implies that the standards in question are airy and ethereal as well as high and pretentious) and of dubious decorum ("not exactly demure" implies that the couple should have been "demure," or perhaps even embarrassed, about enunciating their "lofty standards"). Here is the description: "Emblematic of the Clarkson-Saul aesthetic is the townhouse they share in Toronto's Yorkville district, the city's boutiquey hub. Elegant and casual it is, too—perhaps too studiedly casual?—the centrepiece being the downstairs living room with its walls covered in peachy-pink Thai silk. The art is both figurative and abstract, both sensual and austere. Near the fireplace stands a plaster-of-Paris nymph, picked up at a Paris flea market during the time they lived there in the mid '80s when Clarkson was Ontario's agent-general. The nymph's well-formed backside is illuminated by a tiny spotlight."

Again, we are given the paradox of contrived naturalness—"studiedly casual." Again, we are referred to the suspiciously fashionable—here "boutiquey"—address. The Clarkson-Saul living room, however, despite its casualness, sounds almost like an art gallery. Lownsbrough seems unaware of the furniture, remarking only on the silk-covered walls, the art, and the gallery-style lighting of the statue's backside. By lingering in his description on that backside and the tiny spotlight, he isolates that detail and allows its implied pretentiousness—museum-quality taste—to become the dominant impression. These are some of the lofty things that self-styled sophisticates do, Lownsbrough suggests: they pick up "nymphs" in Paris, they shine arty spotlights on the butts of flea-market statues.

Clarkson's actual body is not present in the scene, but the female body still dominates the description. The walls are "dressed" in "Thai silk." The female statue—a "nymph," in Lownsbrough's estimation—is strongly sexualized, her backside accentuated both by the lighting and Lownsbrough's writing. The backside is "well-formed," evidently much larger than the tiny and arguably male spotlight that allows Lownsbrough to gaze at it.

These various descriptions of Clarkson's living quarters emphasize their abnormality—their elite addresses, their upward mobility, their arty ambiances designed more for gazing at rare objects than for living, their pervasive evocation of the decorative and decadent power of Clarkson's "sophisticated" sexuality. As well, the descriptions subtly—or, in the case of McCracken, not so subtly—chastise Clarkson for having such a narcissistic concern with how others view her self and her world. All the writers seem naively unaware of how normal such a concern is.

Consciousness of how others regard our actions and appearances is fundamental to our social relationships, and many psychological theorists regard it as the most important consequence of the mirror stage, during which humans pass from infancy into self-awareness. People who develop little or no awareness of being perceived by others are considered autistic and are often unable to manage even the simplest of relationships or learn enough language to communicate.

But the primary focus of all four journalists is, as it should be, on the way in which the packaging is done, and on the implied audience of the packaging—that is, who are Clarkson and Saul trying to impress? Breslin hints that Clarkson may be so self-absorbed that her main audience is herself. McCracken knows that this audience is neither Melinda McCracken nor the people with whom she usually associates; she seems to suspect that it may be the Clarkson's wealthy Rosedale neighbours and fellow Liberal-party operatives. Kareda, with his sly humour and his announced awareness that he knows the rooms are only a stage, also places himself outside the intended audience. Partly following Breslin, he makes a more damaging suggestion about the intended audience: that it may be Clarkson and Saul themselves, that the decor may be designed to convince them of their own importance, of their imperial quality. He doesn't describe the couple's guests gazing at the apartment's splendours. Instead, he tells us that the guests gaze at the performing Clarkson, and he portrays the apartment as an extension of Clarkson's person, its "flawless" living room enacting her own "flawless sense of drama." It seems to Kareda that the couple dwells inside Clarkson's own architecturally extended sexuality.

Lownsbrough also dissociates himself from the intended audience of the room he describes, beginning the process with the announcement that the room symbolizes the couple's "lofty" aesthetics, which are both above his own aesthetics and beyond what he can respect. By locating the townhouse in Toronto's "boutiquey hub," he further distances himself, suggesting not only that he is unimpressed by that hub but also that the townhouse itself is "boutiquey"—or flashy and commercially glamorous. His sense of the Clarkson-Saul living room is that it is attention-seeking, it announces that it desires an audience, it wants to impress. The art tries to be everything to all people— "sensual," "austere," "abstract," "figurative." Directing their spotlight at the nymph's derriere, which is—like that of *The Woman*, seen by Breslin—a stand-in for Clarkson's derriere, Clarkson and Saul use the room mischievously to moon their guests. But Lownsbrough refuses to be mooned.

The "boutiquey" Yorkville house and the issue of where the light shines made another public appearance during the year before Clarkson's appointment. Toronto papers reported that Clarkson and Saul had persuaded Toronto City Council to pass an interim control bylaw on all properties in their Yorkville neighbourhood. They were seeking to prevent their next-door neighbour, Katherine Stewart, from constructing an addition to her house. Stewart, the elderly widow of an Ontario lieutenant governor and a former friend of Clarkson's, was in failing health. The addition she wanted to construct was similar to the one that Clarkson and Saul had been permitted to construct on their property in 1989, but Stewart's addition would, *Globe and Mail* reporter Guy Abbate quoted Saul as saying, "cut off light" to the Clarkson-Saul garden. The newspaper reports implied that Clarkson and Saul were the type of people who would bully a frail old woman, betray a friendship, selfishly and undemocratically refuse a neighbour privileges they had enjoyed themselves. After

Clarkson's appointment, the news emerged that the dispute had been abruptly settled and that Mrs. Stewart had died, leaving the property to her son, Alastair Mackay. But in some newspapers the implications remained decidedly negative. In the *Montreal Gazette*, Natalie Armstrong suggested that Clarkson settled to avoid the bad publicity that her new position would draw to the case. She also implied that Clarkson had already unjustly exercised her considerable influence: "'It was just a nasty woman exercising her political powers to make everybody's life miserable. It was a personal vendetta,' said Sasha Jusipovicz, Mackay's designer . . . 'She wanted to be the one who rules Yorkville.' He said the delay meant Mackay's terminally ill mother, Katherine Mackay Stewart, could not spend her last Christmas in the renovated Victorian home that she co-owned with her son and family. She died of cancer last spring at age 85."

Armstrong quotes Clarkson's lawyer, Alan Heisey, but his remarks were scarcely helpful: "Heisey said Ralston Saul has written many books in his office at the couple's champagne-pink home (which now has an RCMP guard on the front porch when Clarkson is in town). He was worried it would have less light if the originally planned addition were build. Clarkson added to her home some time ago, including a conservatory where she grows flowers. 'Madame Clarkson grows orchids, which would also have been significantly impacted in terms of light and shadowing,' said Heisey."

Although many Canadians grow orchids, it is still generally perceived as a leisure-class pursuit. The connotations that Armstrong's story attaches to Heisey's intervention—through the words "champagne" and "conservatory" and the implied pun on "pink champagne"—create a general impression of the house as a site of effete and idle luxury. Heisey's comments about Saul's writing hint that Saul may be a tender prima donna who can perform only in the most protected of environments.

One implication of all this was that Clarkson and Saul belong in a museum or on a theatre set—and, of course, Rideau Hall, the governor-general's residence, is both of these. Another implication was that Clarkson would inevitably—even unconsciously—need to redecorate her official residence. And indeed, with Clarkson's appointment, journalists did turn their attention to the costly splendours of that mansion, and to the appropriateness of its new inhabitants. *Frank* magazine fantasized a one-hundred-thousand-dollar renovation of the hall's private kitchen (the publicly reported cost was forty-two thousand) and new upholstery "of the finest silk, ringing in at over $300 a square metre . . . in keeping with Her Excellency's uncompromising tastes." *Frank* added that Clarkson considered the previous upholstery work, overseen by earlier viceregal spouse Gerda Hnatyshyn, to have reflected "the taste of a Saskabush cowgirl" and that "Once again, La Adrienne is correct" ("Shopaholic GG").

Most journalists agreed that the upper-class tastes of the couple corresponded in some appropriate way to the lavishness of Rideau Hall's spaces and decorations. But they disagreed on what this meant. Some saw the correspondence as ironic and thought that it disqualified Clarkson as a suitable appointee by revealing that she was too patrician to be acceptable; she would be too comfortable in Rideau Hall. Robert Fife, for example, titled an article "Clarkson Warned to Be More Frugal as New Viceroy," and he cited her numerous expense claims for limousines and lunches with friends while she was chair of the Museum of Civilization. Others saw the correspondence as positive—the hall would at last get inhabitants equal to its style. "A Sense of Panache at Rideau Hall," was the title of Rosemary Sexton's enthusiastic column in the Liberal-supporting *Toronto Star*. The *Vancouver Sun*'s Lawrence Martin titled his supportive article "The Price We Pay for Quality." And in the *Globe and Mail*, Michael Valpy wrote, "It is easily imaginable that Rideau Hall with Ms. Clarkson and Mr. Saul in residence will become a salon of the arts and ideas, comparable to the Kennedy White House. The place used to be like that."

Victim of Racism

OR: Victim of Sexism

Whatever Class Advantages

> Indeed, she is remarkably poised, and consistently calm and composed. These are rare qualities, and they incite envy, that most corrosive and ugly deadly sin. (Mel Watkins)

Perhaps it is time I formally introduced myself, the bearded white guy sitting at his computer in humid southwestern Ontario amid several thousand newspaper clippings, photocopies, Internet printouts, and photos of the celebrated and/or philosophical Mr. and Mrs. G.G.

My life has roughly paralleled that of Ms. Clarkson. I was born in Vancouver in 1940, shortly before the outbreak of the conflicts that would cause two-year-old Adrienne Poy and her family to flee across the Pacific to Canada. Among my first memories are blackout curtains on the windows of my home, and the sound of air-raid sirens being tested in case of attacks on our Fraser Valley village and its large Commonwealth air-training field. Attacks by the carrier-based Japanese planes that had bombed Pearl Harbour and assisted in the capture of Poy's Hong Kong. Early village fears of the global village. Nevertheless, one of my cousins did indeed die when his Halifax crashed in the Black Forest. I can remember the *Vancouver Sun* arriving with headlines about the sinking of the *Repulse* and the *Prince of Wales*. And then about Hiroshima.

I took piano lessons and by fourteen could play Schubert impromptus, but I preferred playing "Rock Around the Clock" in a band. Like Clarkson, I was public-speaking champion of my high school and placed second, also like her, in the regional finals. One of my high school badminton partners had been interned during the war because he was Japanese Canadian. At seventeen, I also graduated precociously from high school and was sent by my hopeful non-university-graduate parents to university in Vancouver. My father drove a truck for the province's electric utilities company, the B.C. Electric Company, later nationalized as B.C. Hydro. I lived comfortably—as far as I knew—in a rented basement room, cooking my own meals. My tuition fees were defrayed by B.C. Electric Company scholarships. In the first summers, I worked in the hop fields near Chilliwack, and later I read meters for B.C. Electric. My dad helped me get the job. A patronage appointment.

At the university, I encountered students from wealthy families who were able to take years off to travel, but such luxury was unimaginable to me or my family. I checked. During the 1958 election, I went door-to-door campaigning for Douglas Jung so he could become or remain the first Chinese Canadian member of Parliament. That was my last indirect or direct association with a

Tory. Like Clarkson, I began graduate studies in English; but I started immediately after graduation, because I needed the sixteen hundred dollars per year that a teaching assistantship provided. Like most young men of the time, I had married a woman whose earning potential was lower than my own. Unlike Clarkson, I continued in graduate school, completing my doctorate in 1968. This probably had a lot to do with the fact that I was male and received the cultural encouragements and confirmations that young men then received, but that Adrienne Clarkson *did not*. I bought my first house in 1968. It cost an enormous $21,000. My wife and I divorced, and I remarried. Twelve years later, I made my first overseas trip—to Britain and India.

I've also had a series of jobs financed by public budgets. I began teaching at Royal Roads Military College, in Victoria, in 1963. Women in those decades were not allowed to teach in Canada's military colleges. From 1969 to 1970, I was writer in residence at Sir George Williams University in Montreal. From 1970 to 1990, I taught in the English department at York University, becoming department chair in 1985. In 1986, I supervised Glenn Deer's PhD thesis on class in Canadian fiction, and I hadn't a clue that he was even one-percent Chinese. Since 1990, I have been Carl F. Klinck Professor of Canadian Literature at the University of Western Ontario. Elite positions. Klinck is now a dead white male, like I'll be someday. I have had friends, like Mike Ondaatje and Matt Cohen, who later became friends of Clarkson and Saul. I have published a lot of books—more than thirty—and edited even more books for the "arty" Coach House Press. I've spent most of my life in or near Toronto, but I have never met Madame Clarkson. I twice made academic visits to France while she was my agent general. I was unaware that there was an author named Mr. Saul until Greg Curnoe's widow, Sheila, gave me one of his books,

Reflections of a Siamese Twin. I didn't read it because I thought the title was insensitive to aboriginals and multiculturalism.

I have a big Victorian house that my late wife chose. I live alone in it with two Great Danes that sleep on the furniture. One of them—Stevie—has chewed some of the Victorian woodwork. I dust and vacuum every few months, but things just get dusty again. I have two adult children: a daughter who works in computer software and a son who works in a genetics lab. They occasionally visit me. I like that.

I wonder whether I would have liked Ms. Clarkson. I have noticed that most of the people who dislike her have been, like me, more advantaged than she has been in race and gender, but less advantaged in class and region.

In my childhood village, having a front door on one's house was a sign of class. Having steps that led up to it was slightly better. Actually using the steps and door from time to time was really classy. I still tend to enter my house from the back.

What one did with one's living room was also pretty important. Using it regularly was a huge sign of being common. Having clear plastic covers on the sofa and chairs was so classy it was rumoured that only city folk could have them. The parents of one of my friends strung a velvet rope across the entrance to their living room, just like the ones I later saw across the doorways of period-furnished rooms at Versailles. No one in my village had seen Versailles, but we had seen similar ropes—like the one across the entrance to the dining room at Eaton's. That was one impressive rope. I'll bet there are ropes like that at Rideau Hall.

Refinement meant never eating in the dining room, except on Christmas Day and special birthdays. It meant that at dinnertime, instead of having one glass filled with green onions in the centre of the kitchen table, each person had his or her own glass with onions standing in it. It meant that the kitchen table was chrome and arborite instead of just wood. Eating a green onion with a knife and fork instead of dipping it in salt and biting off a chunk was so refined no one has yet thought of it—until me, right now.

For a kid, class meant that your dad had a car. And clean hands. It meant a collar on your dog. It meant that you could buy a paper Halloween costume. It meant having small metal toys or dimes baked into your birthday cake for your friends to break their teeth on. It meant your dad didn't go hunting. It meant your mom sometimes wore a nylon dress and heels.

When my dad wanted to dress up, he took off his denim work shirt and put on a print shirt and bolo tie. His best bolo tie had a big purply polished agate. For really special occasions, like weddings or barn dances, he had a plaid sports jacket and a wide tie on which a very talented person had painted a rainbow trout. My mom would wear her blue taffeta blouse, onto which she'd sewn a thousand sequins. I bought my first classy thing when I was fourteen. A pair of pink suede shoes. Sure wish I still had them! But I think I'm getting a long way from Adrienne Clarkson.

I was invited to Rideau Hall once, in 1970. I rented a suit and bought a tie that I still have. I couldn't find my pink suede shoes. My wife, Linda, accompanied me. But Linda, who grew up in the city and was much more refined than I, scoffed down all the caviar she could find and I've never been invited back. This is true.

I sometimes take more than a passing interest in politics. Like one of Saul's "mediocre frightened academics." I wrote a book about Kim Campbell because I thought she would campaign as a witty, attractive woman, and she might win another Tory landslide. I wasted my time: she campaigned like an old Tory man.

She forgot that what had made her image interesting was that she seemed hip and a little bit cultured, unlike her colleagues. But a lot like Adrienne Clarkson.

And a lot of people do like Adrienne Clarkson—eighty-seven percent of Canadians, according the October 1999 COMPASS poll. But what does it matter? What does it matter that "sophisticated," Hong Kong-born, francophile, veteran CBC broadcaster, and workaholic Adrienne Clarkson is now governor general of Canada?

And why am I asking? As many politicians have claimed, her appointment had (or had "only") symbolic value—the symbolic value of adding to the characterization of Canada as a diverse, open, multicultural society. Did the appointment accomplish this? Not directly—although national symbolism can cause people to act *as if* things have changed. And by so doing bring about such change. But it could also act as a kind of placebo, or even a sedative: Canadians see that extreme diversity has reached one of the nation's highest offices and ask themselves how much more open the nation needs to become.

Some, however, argue that the nation is now too open. Journalist and photographer Rick McGinnis criticizes a remark of John Ralston Saul's but frames his objections to include Clarkson, describing Saul as the man who hoped to "become Canada's court philosopher when his journalist wife, Adrienne Clarkson, was appointed Governor General of Canada." McGinnis emphasizes that Clarkson is in his view "merely" a journalist, and Saul is someone who would like to be seen as a philosopher. The Saul remark that upsets McGinnis is from *Reflections of a Siamese Twin*: "Canadian culture is the vision of a northern people who, despite substantial and constant difficulties, found a way to live together while other nations tore themselves apart and imposed monolithic, centralized mythologies on themselves." McGinnis doesn't dispute the truth of this remark, but he unhappily observes that for him and many others it is not "attractive." He calls Saul's assertion, "a fairly belligerent way of recycling the old 'Canada is a virtuous absence' school of identity. In a nutshell, a combination of ethnic diversity, regionalism, and the constant challenges to identity provided by waves of immigration have prevented Canada from becoming a xenophobic monoculture; we have, instead, developed a fluid, almost abstract sense of ourselves, something that might not be apparent or even attractive to fishermen in the Maritimes, farmers in Saskatchewan, Innu in the north, or loggers in B.C., but which appeals mightily to newspaper columnists and academic conference organizers. It's a benign, nearly abstract national mythology embraced and promoted by intellectuals like Mr. Saul starting in the Sixties, when the 'good colonial nation' mythology that used to define Canada was becoming not only untrue but unpopular."

McGinnis declares nostalgia for a Canada that was imaginatively a monoculture (the Canada of my parents' green onions?), and he links this view to older, rural, resource-based cultures—those of fishermen, farmers, loggers, and Innu. The new, "abstract" identity he links not only to urban intellectuals but also to "immigration" and "ethnic diversity." As well, he deploys class indicators in this nostalgia: working-class visions of the nation as a monoculture are simple, concrete, and good; educated-class visions of Canada as diverse are complicated, abstract, and bad. He also believes that he detects some sloppy thinking in Saul's identification of nations that "tore themselves apart" in order to become culturally "monolithic" as mostly European nation-states; he suggests that the United States or Japan could also match such a description. McGinnis's reference to Japan reminds his readers that white European nations have not had a monopoly on racism or imperialist ambition and implies that Saul is perhaps being racialist if he believes so. It's a curious and defensive reference. It indicates that McGinnis knows his remarks could be construed as a defence of racism and hopes that a vague reference to Japanese racist nationalism will somehow protect him.

In sharp contrast to McGinnis, others have argued that Clarkson's appointment, far from confirming Canadian diversity, has marked and revealed boundaries in Canadian diversity. One of these people is Glenn Deer. He insists that the appointment shows how someone of non-European ancestry can occupy a position such as that of governor general only within a "multi-cultural" nationalist politic; this politic requires that the candidate agree that her race, and her initial abjection on the basis of race, are two of her major qualifications for the position. According to Deer, the prime minister's statement that the appointment shows "how much our country has matured" reveals that white Europeanness is still, despite this maturing, the cultural norm. Clarkson's friend Margaret Atwood argues that media reactions to the appointment reveal the boundaries still placed around women. Alluding to the news stories that focused on Clarkson's marriages, her estrangement from her children, her ambition, and her treatment of her Yorkville neighbour, Atwood declares, "She's been given a scandalous, rocky ride in the press. It's really been horrible up to now. And they would never do that to a man . . . She's had some press that I'd consider basically sexist and racist" (Sidebar).

For Atwood, the word "racist" here is an afterthought, one that intensifies the accusation of gender discrimination. Her implication is that the media reaction reveals that women are still expected to be faithful wives, devoted mothers, congenial colleagues, and generous neighbours, while men's transgressions of such norms are considered unremarkable. Margaret is pretty sharp.

In one of a handful of scholarly responses to Clarkson's appointment, Andil Gosine attempted to sort out for readers of the journal *Canadian Women's Studies* the signs of gender, race, and nation that the appointment set into play. However, Gosine himself immediately set additional signs into play in his opening paragraph by recalling that as a child he had flipped past Clarkson's television programs because they seemed "in equal parts dull and pretentious." He added that as an adult, before the appointment, he hadn't known that Clarkson "was 'Chinese'"; he was "surprised" to learn that she was. Here again is the Clarkson whose appointment may be objectionable because she is "pretentious." Moreover, Gosine is not making this observation as a cover for sexism or racism—as Atwood implies most media critics of Clarkson had done. Instead, his is the spontaneous, "childhood" (and therefore implicitly "pure") response of someone who (like Atwood) disdains sexism and racism. And here again is the "not very Chinese" characterization of Clarkson, with its implied accusation that she had been able to pass as white, that Jan Wong and Glenn Deer articulated, in contrasting ways, and that earlier commentators like Breslin had resorted to when they expressed surprise at Clarkson's occasional flashes of "Chineseness." Hidden beneath these observations are such statements as, "pretty good for a Chinese," or, "really good for a Chinese," with their double signalling first of a Canadian racism that makes Asian success in Canada difficult, and second of an unexplained, presumably innate, Asian handicap.

Next, Gosine surveys responses to the appointment. "We were told about her failed first marriage and her quickie new one, her 'tragic' estrangement from her daughters, her uppity ways, and exorbitant spending habits, and her harassment of one neighbour." He quotes some of the negative responses—those of Winsor, Fotheringham, and Connie Woodcock—that strongly invoke race and imply that Clarkson's Chineseness alone earned her the viceregal position. He concludes not only that both "the 'negative' and 'positive' reactions to her appointment invoke race and gender in inventing the nation of Canada," but also that all of the negative reactions—to her ambitiousness, uppitiness, unmotherliness, or reliance on her husband—are codes for racism. Asian women, Gosine insists, have generally been associated in North America with such stereotypes. Yoko Ono was perceived as a parasite on the talent of John Lennon, Imelda Marcos was perceived as too tastelessly pretentious to deserve wealth, the character Ling on television's *Ally McBeal* is portrayed as "callous, manipulative, and unemotionally attached."

Gosine also points out that the combination of welcoming Clarkson to the governor general's post because she is Chinese and female and lamenting her appointment because the choice of a Chinese woman "degrades Her Majesty, the office of Governor General and Canada as a whole" (Kenneth Lieblich, a former officer of the Monarchist League of Canada, quoted in Brooke), reinforces "sexist and racist relations of power in Canada." For Gosine, this confirms that white men still constitute the nation, and that women and nonwhites can at best be nonconstituting symbols of the nation's ethical qualities—its motherly goodness, decency, inclusiveness, and diversity. Through her appointment,

Gosine conjectures, Clarkson has become the symbolic mother of multicultural Canada, and for this reason, her personal tragedy as a mother is psychologically significant to many of her detractors: that is, calling her a "bad (biological) mother" undermines her suitability to be the symbolic mother of the nation. Moreover, Gosine reflects, it was appropriate that Clarkson was appointed "to a symbolic post like the governor general," because such a functionally limited post demonstrates how women in national governmental positions still play roles that are more symbolic (of national gender "fairness") than they are functional.

Clarkson's subsequent performance of such a conventionally motherly role—encouraging Canadians to be proud of their accomplishments in political compromise, bilingualism, tolerance, and "forgiving"; framing these qualities within a discourse of nationalism as characteristically "Canadian" accomplishments—lends considerable credence to Gosine's analysis. So, too, do the loud objections made by many Canadians whenever Clarkson appears to overstep her symbolic role and attempt to influence government policy. These objectors find it acceptable for Clarkson to offer comforting platitudes or performative statements of symbolic desire, as she did during her installation speech when she invited Canadians to "embark on a journey" with her. But they consider it unacceptable for her to declare poverty shameful or charity demeaning, or to praise bilingualism excessively, because to do so presumes a power and agency unbefitting an "uppity" governor general.

Something of a problem in Gosine's analysis, however, is the way in which it subsumes all of the criticisms of Clarkson within the categories of race and gender. Canadians are also extremely sensitive to class and regional differences, and these sensitivities have been intensely visible in the various reactions to Clarkson throughout her career. Gosine mentions class only to brush it off, saying of Clarkson, "her personal achievements are quite remarkable, whatever class advantages she possessed." However, to claim that the hostile portrayal of Clarkson as "uppity" has been based only on prejudices about gender and race is to ignore the strong class-based uneasiness that has informed most commentary on Clarkson since the late 1960s. Both Catherine Breslin in 1969 and Melinda McCracken in 1972 were much more conscious of Clarkson's Upper Canada connectedness and her educated cosmopolitan tastes than they were of her Chineseness, and they seem to have included that Chineseness within Clarkson's easy cosmopolitanism rather than resenting her cosmopolitanism because she was Chinese. Their sense that Clarkson's self-invented upper-class grandeur was alien to ordinary Canadians like themselves, that it made her appear to inhabit a parallel universe of European holidays, fine paintings, and instant gratification, reemerged in Kareda's impressions of her regal expectations. It came up, as well, in the amused remarks of the various commentators who thought that Clarkson's viceregal appointment was ironically appropriate. Deborah Grey's awkward attempts to joke about Clarkson's wish to be called "Madame" reflected working-class humour much more than it reflected any subliminal associations of Asian women with prostitution. The various "Queen Adrienne" epithets may have been partly prompted by Canadian racism, but they had at least as much do with class issues: with Canadian resentment towards remittance men in the nineteenth century, and towards plummy English accents in the last century; with support for the 1919 Nickle Resolution's abolition of noble titles for Canadians; and with support for Jean Chrétien's refusal to allow Conrad Black to be both "Lord Black" and Canadian.

Canadian perceptions of the arts as upper-class enthusiasms, and of the CBC as the chosen broadcaster of educated and privileged Canadians, were also active in the negative responses to Clarkson. So was class resentment that the publicly funded CBC and Canadian Museum of Civilization appear mainly to serve those who are privileged by education and who can claim refinement of taste. One persistent complaint in the year before her appointment was that Clarkson had routinely used her Museum of Civilization expense account to travel by "limousine," to stay at "the well-appointed Chateau Laurier," and to entertain at elegant restaurants not only friends (such as Margaret Atwood, CBC colleagues Kelly Crichton and Susan Teskey, and her sister-in-law Vivienne Poy), but also "powerful figures in the Liberal Government" (McGregor). Again, it is difficult to see how race could play a dominant role in perceptions that Clarkson was funding a lavish and "arty" lifestyle with public money. Gender may have played a role, since one of the prevailing stereotypes of the arts is that they are feminine, that male artists are effeminate, and that the audiences for ballet and opera are mostly female. That stereotype was visible in many of the early characterizations of John Ralson Saul as a prima donna for whom ordinary Perrier water was not good enough, or as a francophile dandy who affectedly displayed silk handkerchiefs and sported designer clothing.

Yet gender does not appear to have played much of a role in the later characterizations of Saul as "a patrician of humble origins," "an arrogant, self-serving blowhard," or "an ill-humoured, elitist Rex Murphy"; neither does it seem to have been important to those who expressed their unhappiness at Saul's assuming the routine spousal title of Excellency. Moreover, the fact that accusations of elitism were directed as much at Saul, and at the perceived arrogance of his cultural writings, as at Clarkson suggests that both racism and gender were lesser factors than class. Even Atwood's claim that criticisms of Clarkson were sexist and racist can easily be interpreted as yet another elitist's unwillingness to acknowledge that well-educated, well-connected, and accomplished Canadians can be the targets of class envy.

Regional Canadian antipathies, especially towards Ontario and its presumptions of economic and cultural leadership, were particularly evident in the negative responses to Clarkson's appointment. The vast majority of the characterizations of Clarkson as haughty and vainglorious originated in Western Canada, especially in the Calgary newspapers. These much more strongly associated her with the CBC, with Ottawa, with Toronto, and with her Yorkville "salon" than they did with her gender and race. As governor general, Clarkson has, if anything, confirmed such an association. Her cultural reference points have continued to be central Canadian, with the occasional token reference to someone like Robert Kroetsch or Antonine Maillet. Northrop Frye, an Ontario imperialist in the eyes of many literary people in Western Canada, has continued to be the Canadian writer she quotes most frequently.

For those who celebrated Clarkson's appointment, her prime symbolic values were class and culture. The arts were at last going to get an high profile in official Ottawa, and Canadian writers and artists would be given awards by someone whose understanding of the arts was wider and more complex than knowing how to sing "When Irish Eyes Are Smiling" in the National Arts Centre. To her new office, Clarkson was going to impart "panache" (Sexton and McIlroy), "élan" (Winsor), "dash" (McIlroy); she and Saul would "bring back the pomp of the old court." They would rescue "the term 'intellectual' from its dirty-word status" (Martin, "But Watch"). This was a strong response, and it cropped up in all of the national papers, whatever their ideological partisanship. While it may have been inflected by the popular gendering of the arts as female, it was again directed almost as much at Saul as at Clarkson.

A number of people who were not directly associated with the arts had the same response, often expressing pleasure in the kind of international symbol of Canada that Clarkson would make. There were echoes here of the perception shared by many Canadians that Pierre Elliott Trudeau had been an effective symbol of Canada abroad—that he had given others the impression that Canadians were bilingual, articulate, intelligent, well educated, cultured, stylish, and creative. This impression, of course, was somewhat inaccurate, but it was no less inaccurate than other shorthand symbolic representations of the country have been. In Clarkson's case, the symbolism was also going to be highly idealized—her implied Canadians would be bilingual, articulate, intelligent, well educated, cultured, stylish, creative, *and* racially diverse and gender neutral.

But again, it is difficult to argue that race and gender dominate in this constellation of symbolic qualities, although there is considerable interaction. The value of the bilingualism is enhanced when it is a person of Asian ancestry who has achieved fluency in both official languages—the Asian individual appears to be saluting and endorsing "original" English-French Canadianness. Similarly, the value of a broad knowledge of Western cultural history and the ability to appear cultured and stylish in Western terms seems aggrandized when the person who possesses these aptitudes is Asian-born. Considering the systemic disadvantaging of women in almost all societies, the overall mix of qualities and abilities is perhaps, in Western culture, marginally more impressive in a woman than a man. But it is also not unusual. As well, people's perceptions of gender and race themselves are qualified in the case of Clarkson by the other symbolic qualities, which have expanded, for example, what "Asian" or "Chinese" can signify—much the way people's cultural perceptions of race have been altered by the virtuosity of musicians like Wynton Marsalis, Midori, and Seiji Ozawa.

Significantly, Trudeau also attracted proportionally more hostility in Western Canada than he did in Ontario, and not only because of his National Energy Program. There were strong elements of regional suspicion in such responses, of west versus east, and of class-based suspicion of high culture; Trudeau's pirouettes, fashionable clothing, bilingualism, and occasional squiring of classical guitarist Liona Boyd all contributed to this suspicion. Clarkson would likely have been the focus of similar suspicion, though possibly not as strong, even if she wasn't Asian and female.

Yet racist hostility towards Clarkson was definitely present. The racist hostility of Canada First's Paul Fromm was explicit, even though he overlapped it with some less obviously racist objections. Like mainstream newspaper reporters, and like Jean Chrétien, Fromm considered Clarkson's appointment to be symbolic of Canada's developing diversity and her racial background to be one of the attributes she brought to the position. But instead of using positive phrases like Chrétien's "an indication of how much our country has matured," he characterized the appointment as "a good way to show traditional Canadians who was in charge." He thus showed how easily racialized perceptions such as Chrétien's can be translated into something overtly racist. "We opposed the appointment of Chinese immigrant Adrienne Clarkson from the beginning," wrote Fromm. "The woman had no discernible public service merit to make her an obvious candidate for the office. In politically correct Ottawa, making a Chinese woman Governor General would be a good way to show traditional Canadians who was in charge and it was not they! Clarkson is a potent symbol (and insult!) of the dispossession and replacement of traditional Canadians by a new multicult order."

Fromm's statement also overlaps with the subtle or perhaps unconscious racism of McGinnis's distinction between old and therefore fondly remembered Canadians (like fishermen and loggers) and "waves of immigration." Fromm identifies Clarkson as a "Chinese immigrant," signalling his unwillingness to give her credit for any years of Canadian citizenship. As well, he distinguishes her from "traditional Canadians," who, if anything, are not Chinese. Clarkson and her Chineseness are "an insult"— presumably to "traditional Canadians"—Fromm writes, echoing Lieblich's viciously racist contention that Clarkson's appointment "degrades Her Majesty, the office of Governor General and Canada as a whole." His argument that Clarkson has "no discernible public service merit" echoes the arguments put forward by a number of mainstream media commentators, who maintained that her lack of experience as an elected politician was regrettable. Overall, Fromm's statement demonstrates how such weak, petty, or desperate objections to Clarkson's appointment—that she had never been elected, that she had deserted her children, that she had made life difficult for her elderly neighbour, that she had written poor novels, that she had expensive tastes—can be read as signs that the writer's actual objection is the unspeakable one of race.

In their extreme overstating of the differences between the immigrant and "traditional Canadians," and in their characterization of Chineseness as part of a "new multicult order," Fromm's remarks also suggest that objections to multiculturalism, such as those made with regards to the appointment by *Vancouver Sun* and *National Post* writers, could also conceal unacknowledged or unconscious racism. Multiculturalism is a policy that can be rationally debated, refused, or chosen. But it does not—as Fromm implies—exclude any Canadians, even "traditional" ones. His claims to the contrary appeared in a still more extreme and revealing form on the Web site of the self-declared anti-Semitic American group the Vanguard News Network. Here the headline was even more overstated—"The Horror of Multiculturalism Personified"—and refugee Clarkson became a "slant-eyed" child "who grew up on some overcrowded sampan near a sewage outfall" and who in Canada had "stolen a White woman's pretty name" (I am quoting only the most polite of Web site's characterizations). Again, one can see how petty objections—Wong's to the fact that Clarkson retained her first husband's name—or invented ones—such as Bourette and Milner's that Clarkson's daughters would "shun" and "boycott" her installation—are very similar in kind to racism because racism itself does not rest on substantial arguments.

Senator Pat Carney encountered a related phenomenon in preparing her memoir, *Trade Secrets*, for publication in 2000. Carney thought that the grey dress Clarkson wore to open the fall 1999 session of Parliament was unbecoming, and she'd written that it "made her look like a washerwoman." Her publisher asked her to change the passage, "because it suggests all Chinese Canadians worked in Chinese laundries." Carney remarked, "I was mystified. China-born myself, I had many Canadian Chinese friends and not one of them, nor their families, had ever worked in a Chinese laundry. The Governor-General comes from a distinguished Chinese family, much more prestigious than mine."

Here, again, the criticism of Clarkson is petty, and one could easily read the fact that it was being made at all as a sign that the writer had other criticisms of Clarkson that she was not prepared to articulate. But the criticism was also connected to cultural signs of racism that are embedded in the English language—signs such as the word "inscrutable," which had betrayed Breslin's uneasiness with Clarkson's Chineseness. For Carney, the "washer-woman" simile consciously invoked class. In her own defence, she wrote that she had borrowed the image from her husband, who had said that the dress reminded him of a "char-lady charac-ter" played by Carol Burnett. Sophisticated Adrienne had dressed like a lowly servant. But Chinese immigrants to Canada have also been associated with images of low-class servitude, notably with the washing of wealthy people's clothes—as Carney's easy access to the phrase "Chinese laundry" confirms. The racial stereotyping that Carney had unwittingly performed had, in a sense, been written for her, or written onto her, by the English language.

Clarkson herself has rarely made an issue of her encounters with racism, and in her official speeches she usually congratulates Canadians on being diverse and welcoming. But she did acknowl-edge Canadian racism when speaking at a 2000 University of Toronto convocation during which Desmond Tutu was given an honorary degree. Student and *Varsity* newspaper reporter Jesse Clark was so surprised to witness this that he wrote, "Even Adrienne Clarkson mentioned racism in Canada." Another exception had occurred in 1991. In an address to the Urban Alliance on Race Relations, Clarkson revealed that she had been offended by certain remarks, "couched in a sly manner, asking the reader if they thought my eyes had been altered by plastic surgery." These remarks had been published in *Frank* magazine, and Clarkson had written a letter of protest to the editor. "The implication," she told the Alliance, "that I as a woman could not look the way I do without facial surgery (the racist element aside) was grossly insulting. Misogyny and racism make pretty nasty little bedfellows" ("Frankly").

Perhaps not coincidentally, Clarkson's two strongest speeches as governor general have been on the issue of racism. She delivered both to audiences at high schools where there had been serious incidents of interracial violence. Clarkson gave one of these speeches at Queen Elizabeth Senior Secondary in Surrey, British Columbia, where a fight had broken out between Sikh and white students who were indirectly involved in the trial of five young white men accused of killing the Sikh caretaker of a nearby temple. Over half the students at Queen Elizabeth are of Sikh or Chinese ancestry. Appealing to the example of early B.C. governor James Douglas, who was of a mixed-race background, Clarkson characterized him humanistically as "a man who was a product of muddled colonialism and human instinct." In so doing, she managed both to criticize colonialism and celebrate human biology's ability to overcome prejudice. "What is wonderful about Canada is that it is capable of change," she continued, most likely referring to the symbolism of her own viceregal position (archived speech, 19 Nov. 1999).

Clarkson gave her second strong speech at Nova Scotia's Cole High School. Cole has substantial black and white populations, and it had been the site of several interracial conflicts resulting in injury and criminal charges in the months before Clarkson's visit. Here Clarkson wisely invoked the example of South Africa's Desmond Tutu. Just three days before, she had witnessed Tutu being awarded the honorary degree by the University of Toronto. She referred in detail to his Truth and Reconciliation Commission and the forgiveness of death and torture that it had accomplished, allowing the students of Cole High to understand that their conflicts were a part of much greater and more historic conflicts, which had produced the wisdom of Tutu and Mandela. She also, for once, abandoned some of the congratulatory rhetoric that has marked most of her comments on Canadian diversity. "Racism is no longer institutionalized in our laws," she told the students. "But what we will never be able to do—nor would we want to—is to legislate what people think. We can't forbid the person sitting next to you from having an ugly, dishonest, even perhaps hateful thought. But we can make it socially unacceptable for them to act on those thoughts, to implement hatred. Although racism is not in our laws, it is still out there. There are things that foment hatred among groups. And these days, intolerance can sneak up on you—in the music that you listen to, in videos, on the Internet. I think the very best way to counter these kind of influences is to develop your own skills of communication, to get control" (archived speech, 18 Feb. 2000).

Racism has "sneaked up" on a number of Clarkson's critics, although it would be difficult to determine precisely how many. Clarkson here mentions its seemingly deliberate and conscious manifestations—Internet sites, videos, music. But it is also there in the language we speak, and beneath the petty criticisms people make of nonconformity, exceptionality, bad novel writing, sentimentality, vanity, ambition, and independence.

Canadians do not have to like their governors general. In fact, they have rarely used likeability as a criterion with which to measure one. Members of the British royal family have to be liked, because the survival of their institutions depends upon the public purse and public approbation. Members of the media have to be liked in some way—for their lovableness, irascibility, impetuousness, or rebelliousness—because if their audiences shrink, then so will their incomes. But the question of whether governors general like Romeo Leblanc or Ed Schreyer or Jeanne Sauvé were "likeable" was one that few people considered relevant to their appointments. Why has it become relevant to Adrienne Clarkson's? Possibly because she was already a media personality whose success had depended on being liked. Possibly also because her appointment was announced and greeted with such expectation: she would symbolize a "new" Canada; Rideau Hall would never "be the same."

Those who choose to evaluate Clarkson and Saul on the basis of whether they like them, and who determine the couple's acceptability and worthiness as people on this basis, are saying as much about their own beliefs and feelings as they are about Mr. and Mrs. G.G's. This is equally true of Jan Wong or Melinda McCracken or Margaret Atwood or Mark Steyn. Some of these individuals appear to be pursuing ideological arguments ongoing within their own communities—the Chinese community, the feminist community, the right-wing community—at the expense of the viceregal couple. Clarkson and Saul may not be people whom you or I or Stephen Harper or Melinda McCracken would wish to associate with. I may find his scholarship shallow and her views of the spiritual dimensions of culture quaintly Victorian. I may find his self-absorption and her high-culture attachments pretentious. But that doesn't mean that I should find them unworthy as human beings or fear that she will perform the viceregal role disastrously. The role is, after all, both symbolic and pretentious. It requires—as Kareda noted of the agent-general role—a lot of playacting. It is hortatory, celebratory, performative, and artificial—a five-year episode of *Adrienne Clarkson Presents.*

References

Abbate, Guy. "Clarkson's Neighbours Take Dispute to OMB." *Globe and Mail* 17 May 1999: A7.

Althusser, Louis. *For Marx.* Trans. Ben Brewster. London: New Left, 1977.

——. *Lenin and Philosophy and Other Essays.* Trans. Ben Brewster. New York: Monthly Review, 1971.

Amiel, Barbara. "The Thrill of Discovery." Rev. of *The Birds of Prey*, by John Ralston Saul. *Maclean's* 14 Nov. 1977: 82, 84.

Armour, Leslie. "Woes of Reason." Rev. of *Voltaire's Bastards*, by John Ralston Saul. *Canadian Forum* Mar. 1993: 43–45.

Armstrong, Natalie. "Vice-Regal Appointee Clarkson Ends Backyard Spat." *Gazette* [Montreal] 12 Oct. 1999: A10.

Aspler, Tony. Rev. of *The Next Best Thing*, by John Ralston Saul. *Books in Canada* July 1986: 23.

Atwood, Margaret. *Bodily Harm.* Toronto: McClelland and Stewart, 1981.

Aumon, Ann. "Ontario's Promoter in Paris Pitches for France in Metro." *Toronto Star* 25 Oct. 1983: D8.

Bagehot, Walter. *The English Constitution.* 1867. London: Collins/ Fontana, 1973.

Barthes, Roland. *Mythologies.* 1957. London: Cape, 1972.

Batten, Jack. Rev. of *A Lover More Condoling*, by Adrienne Clarkson. *Saturday Night* May 1968: 37–38.

Bell, Mike. "Krall Claims Success." *Calgary Sun* 13 Oct. 2001: 51.

Beyer, Hubert. "Saul Wades into Political Minefields. *Kimberley Daily Bulletin* 19 Dec. 2001: 4.

Billig, Michael. *Talking of the Royal Family.* London: Routledge, 1992.

Black, Barbara. Rev. of *The Next Best Thing*, by John Ralston Saul. *Gazette* [Montreal] 4 July 1987: J9.

Bloedow, Tim. "Queen Adrienne." *The Interim* Nov. 1999: 5.

Bourdieu, Pierre. *The Rules of Art.* 1992. Stanford: Stanford UP, 1996.

Bourette, Susan, and Brian Milner. "Clarkson's Daughters Will Shun Ceremony." *Globe and Mail* 1 Oct. 1999: A1, A4.

Bourrie, Mark. "John Ralston Saul Sets Table for Lively Appetizing Political Talk." Rev. of *On Equilibrium*, by John Ralston Saul. *Hill Times* 28 Jan. 2002: 13.

Breslin, Catherine. "Adrienne Clarkson: TV's Cool Lady." *Chatelaine* Jan. 1969: 22–23, 67–68, 70.

Brook, Paula. "Part of the Regal Couple's Message Gets Lost in the Lack of Translation." *Vancouver Sun* 24 Nov.1999: A19.

Brooke, James. "Canada's Link to the Queen Grows Livelier." *New York Times* 25 Oct. 1999: A3.

Bryden, Joan. "Clarkson a Governor General 'With Ideas.'" *Calgary Herald* 9 Sept. 1999: A1, A3.

——. "Clarkson New Governor-General." *Gazette* [Montreal] 9 Sept. 1999: A8.

Bunner, Paul. "Our Man in Nirvana." *The Report* 24 Apr. 2000: 34–35.

Cannadine, David. "The Context, Performance, and Meaning of Ritual: The British Royal Family and the 'Invention of Tradition.'" *The Invention of Tradition.* Ed. Eric Hobsbawm and Terence Ranger. Cambridge: Cambridge UP, 1983. 101–64.

Cannon, Margaret. "'Western Literary Elites Will Disappear.'" *Globe and Mail* 10 May 1986: D3.

Cameron, Stevie. "New Publishing Career Takes Clarkson 'Beyond Adrenalin.'" *Globe and Mail* 23 July 1987: A2.

Carey, Elaine. "Clarkson Calls a New Tune at McClelland and Stewart."
    Toronto Star 14 May 1988: M1, M6.

Carney, Pat. "Pitfalls of Political Correctness: Why You Can Hardly
    Write Nothing No More." Speaking notes by the Honourable Pat
    Carney, PC, Senator for British Columbia, to the Media Club of
    Ottawa, 23 Apr. 2001. <www.sen.parl.gc.ca/pcarney/english/
    Archives/Speeches/pol-itical_correctness.htm>

Carson, Susan. "Clarkson: I Want to Make Book Publishing Pay."
    Gazette [Montreal] 7 Dec. 1987: B12.

Cheadle, Bruce. "Are We Getting a 2-for-1 Vice-Regal Deal?" *Gazette*
    [Montreal] 10 Sept. 1999: A8.

Ching, Frank. "Canada Honours a Chinese." *Far Eastern Economic
    Review* 14 Oct. 1999: 31.

"Christmas Traditions Remembered." *Chatelaine* Dec. 1984: 86.

Churchill, David. "The Great National Table." *Vintages* Sept. 2002:
    24–25.

Chwialkowska, Luiza. "Couple Used to Taking Political Centre Stage."
    National Post 9 Sept. 1999: A7.

Clark, Jesse. "South Africa's Bishop Tutu Receives Degree from Uni-
    versity of Toronto." *ePeak News* 28 Feb. 2000. <www.peak.sfu.ca/
    the-peak/2000-1/issue7/tutu.html>

Clarkson, Adrienne. Archived speeches.

——. "Are We Selling Out?" *Homemaker's Magazine* Oct. 1991: 40–41,
    46.

——. "Beginnings." *Today* 13 Sept. 1980: 3.

——. "Counterpoint: Leonard Cohen." *Intricate Preparations: Writing
    Leonard Cohen.* Ed. Stephen Scobie. Toronto: ECW, 2000: 1–2.

——. "Ecological Chic." *Saturday Night* Aug. 1972: 27–29.

——. Foreword. *L.M. Montgomery and Canadian Culture.* Ed. Irene
    Gammel and Elizabeth Epperly. Toronto: U of Toronto P, 1999.
    ix-xii.

——. Foreword. *Celebrating Inuit Art, 1948–70.* Ed. Maria von Fincken-
    stein. Toronto: Key Porter; Ottawa: Canadian Museum of Civili-
    zation, 1999. 8–9.

——. "Frankly Racist." *Currents* 7.1 (1991): 4.

——. *Hunger Trace.* Toronto: McClelland and Stewart, 1970.

——. "If It's Sunday Then This Must Be Inuvik." *Saturday Night* Nov. 1972: 31, 33–34.

——. "Immigration, As It Should Be." *Globe and Mail* 13 Oct. 1997: A15.

——. "An Immigrant's Progress." *Maclean's* 1 July 2001: 26–27.

——. "The Annotated Adrienne Clarkson." Installation Speech. *National Post* 8 Oct. 1999: B10.

——. *A Lover More Condoling.* Toronto: McClelland and Stewart, 1968.

——. "Opinion Platform." *Financial Post* 5 May 1979: 7.

——. "Paris Is a State of Mind." *Canadian Forum* Sept. 1972: 26–28.

——. "A Paris Memo to Lawyers: Toughen Up." *Canadian Lawyer* May 1986: 36, 38–40.

——. "Poor No More: The Chinese in Canada Have Risen from a Despised to a Respected Ethnic Group Through Hard Work and Clannishness." *Today* 7 Nov. 1981: 14–16.

——. "Understanding Hearts: Adrienne Clarkson Goes Home." *Weekend* 29 Sept. 1979: 24–28, 31–38.

——. "We Took a Turbo-Prop on the Golden Road to Samarkand." *Maclean's* Oct. 1968: 4a–4d, 92a–92d.

Clarkson, Adrienne, ed. *True to You in My Fashion.* Toronto: New Press, 1971.

Cohen, Andrew. "Down But Not Out in London and Paris." *Financial Post* 21 Dec. 1985: 19.

COMPASS Inc. "Canada Has a Governor General: Report to the *National Post*." <www.compas.ca/html/archives/gov_gen_surv. html>.

Cooper, Barry, and David Bercuson. "Chrétien Made Mistake in Appointing Clarkson." *Calgary Herald* 15 Sept. 1999: A22.

Coyne, Andrew. "One for the Rosedale Nation." *National Post* 10 Sept. 1999: A15.

Cumming, Don. "The Art of Darkness." Rev. of *The Next Best Thing*, by John Ralston Saul. *Maclean's* 21 Apr. 1986: 69.

Davidson, Dan. "Taking the Measure of the Nation." *Klondike Sun* 31 Mar. 2000: 4.

Deakin, Basil. "TV Hasn't Eaten Adrienne Clarkson Alive." *Chronicle-Herald* [Halifax] 13 May 1978: 8.

REFERENCES

Deer, Glenn. "Asian North America in Transit." *Canadian Literature* 163 (1999): 5–15.

Denley, Randall. "Clarkson Will Enliven Cultural Life." *Ottawa Citizen* 10 Sept. 1999: C4.

Diebel, Linda. "Clarkson Scores Success as Ontario's Paris Agent." *Calgary Herald* 24 June 1986: A5.

Dingman, Jocelyn. "Watch Daytime TV and Be a Geriatric PhD." *Maclean's* Apr. 1967: 110.

Ditchburn, Jennifer. "Governor General Clarkson." *Chronicle-Herald* [Halifax] 9 Sept. 1999: A1, A2.

"Do We Need Women's Lib?" *Chatelaine* Nov. 1970: 27, 82, 84.

Dubé, Francine. "Clarkson, Saul Married in Style." *National Post* 16 Sept. 1999: A7.

Dunn, James. "Male Menopause Mystery a Mix of the Insightful and the Banal." Rev. of *The Paradise Eater*, by John Ralston Saul. *Vancouver Sun* 11 June 1988: E4.

Eagleton, Terry. *Literary Theory: An Introduction.* Oxford: Basil Blackwell, 1983.

Editorial. *Daily Gleaner* [Fredericton] 9 Sept. 1999: 4.

Editorial. *Gazette* [Montreal] 9 Sept. 1999.

"An Excellent Choice." Editorial. *Gazette* [Montreal] 9 Sept. 1999: B2.

Farley, Maggie. "'Outsider' Feeling Right at Home in New Role as Governor General." *Los Angles Times* 25 Dec. 1999.

Fawcett, Brian. Rev. of *The Paradise Eater*, by John Ralston Saul. *Books in Canada* June 1988: 7.

Fescue, Scott. "She's the Governor General. And You're Not." *National Post* 9 Sept. 1999: A1, A6.

Fetherling, Douglas. "Citizen Saul." *Toronto Life* Nov. 1997: 120–24, 126.

Fetherling, George. "A Patrician of Humble Origins." *Vancouver Sun* 26 Jan. 2002: D18.

Fife, Robert. "Activists Move into Rideau Hall." *National Post* 9 Sept. 1999: A1, A6.

——. "Broadcaster Says She and Her Husband Won't Temper Views." *National Post* 9 Sept. 1999: A1.

——. "Clarkson Warned to be More Frugal as New Viceroy." *National Post* 19 Oct. 1999: A4.

——. "For Governor General's Swearing-In Ceremony, Traditions May 'Disappear.'" *National Post* 13 Sept. 1999: A8.

——. "Your Very Own Portrait of Clarkson, Saul for $15,000." *National Post* 20 Oct. 1999: A7.

Fisher, Douglas. "Ask Why, Not How Dare They." *Ottawa Sun* 19 Dec. 2001: 14.

Flohil, Richard. "But Are the Politicians Really Listening, Anyway?" *Canadian Composer* June 1973: 22, 24, 26, 28.

Foot, Richard. "Adrienne Clarkson Is 'Madame,' And You're Not." *National Post* 5 Oct. 1999: A1, A6.

——. "Challenge for Clarkson Is to Win Hearts of Canadians." *National Post* 9 Sept. 1999: A6.

——. "'Embark on a Journey with Me.'" *National Post* 10 Oct. 1999: A1, A2.

——. "Two Homes and a Tax-Free Salary—And the Power to Fire a PM." *National Post* 8 Oct. 1999: A3.

Fotheringham, Allan. "Clarkson Needs Job to Fill in Her Time." *Calgary Herald* 27 Oct. 1985: B1.

——. "Get Her to the Church on Time." *Toronto Sun* 11 Sept. 1999: 15.

——. "Our First Female Prime Minister." *Maclean's* 13 Oct. 1986: 72.

Foucault, Michel. *The Archaeology of Knowledge.* Trans. A.M. Sherian Smith. London: Tavistock, 1972.

Fraser, Graham. "We Want to Keep Monarchy." *Toronto Star* 31 May 2002: A16.

Fraser, John. "Clarkson Wins Kudos Hustling for Ontario." *Globe and Mail* 15 Oct. 1985: A11.

Fromm, Paul. Letter. Dec. 2001. <laurea.topcities.com>

Frye, Northrop. *The Modern Century.* Toronto: Oxford UP, 1967.

Gatehouse, Jonathon. "Broadcaster Has Lived Her Life in the Public Eye." *National Post* 9 Sept. 1999: A3.

Geddes, John. "Inside Track to Our Hijacked Civilization." Rev. of *The Unconscious Civilization*, by John Ralston Saul. *Financial Post* 16 Nov. 1996: 30.

——. "Philosopher King." *Maclean's* 4 Feb. 2002: 58–60.

"Go Ahead, Take the Rest of Your Life Off." Editorial. *Ottawa Citizen* 12 July 1999: A11.

REFERENCES

Gobeil, Charlotte. "Life after Free Trade: An Interview with Adrienne Clarkson." *The New Federation* Jan.-Feb. 1989: 16–18.

Gordon, Charles. "Excellencies." *Ottawa Citizen* 15 Dec. 2001: B6.

Gosine, Andil. "Presenting Adrienne Clarkson: Gender, Nation, and a New Governor-General." *Canadian Women's Studies* 20:2 (2000): 6–10.

Gould, Allan M. "Chatelaine's Celebrity: Adrienne Clarkson." *Chatelaine* Oct.1982: 36.

Greenaway, Norma. "'Visionary' Governor-General Throws Ho-Hum Ottawa a Welcome Curve." *Vancouver Sun* 16 Oct. 1999: B11.

Greenaway, Norma, and Joan Bryden. "Clarkson Welcomed as Break from Political Past." *Vancouver Sun* 9 Sept. 1999: A1, A12.

Grey, Colin. "Left-Leaning Thinker, Often Criticizes Political Elite." *Ottawa Citizen* 9 Sept. 1999: A5.

Harrison, Michael. "Yearning to Escape the Prison of Reason." Rev. of *Voltaire's Bastards*, by John Ralston Saul. *Financial Post* 5 Oct. 1992: F7.

H.T.K. [H.T. Kirkwood]. Rev. of *A Lover More Condoling*, by Adrienne Clarkson. *Canadian Forum* May 1968: 46.

Hornbeck, Paul. "Canadian Causes a Scandal in Paris." *Quill and Quire* Oct. 1977: 19–20.

"The Horror of Multiculturalism Personified." Vanguard News Network. <www.vanguardnews-network.com>

Hoy, Claire. "Vice-Regal." *Sudbury Star* 19 Dec. 2001: A10.

Inness, Lorna. "From Ph.D. Thesis to Best-Selling Thriller." Rev. of *The Birds of Prey*, by John Ralston Saul. *Chronicle-Herald* [Halifax] 13 May 1978: 36.

Janigan, Mary. "Adrienne's Ottawa." *Maclean's* 20 Sept. 1999: 18–21.

Kareda, Urjo. "The Daughter Also Rises." *Saturday Night* June 1986: 30–38.

Kirchoff, H.J. "Thoughts on Escape and the Role of the Novelist." *Globe and Mail* 20 Sept. 1988: A24.

Knox, Jack. "Muzzling Saul Will Solve Nothing." *Victoria Times-Colonist* 15 Dec. 2001: A3.

Korn, Alision. "Sept. 11 'Crystalized Attention': Saul." *Ottawa Citizen* 17 Dec. 2001: A4.

Labreche, Julianne. "Is Beauty a Ticket to Success?" *Chatelaine* Feb. 1982: 60–61, 92–93, 96–97.

Lautens, Stephen. "A Modern Governor General." *Toronto Sun* 15 Oct. 1999: 43.

Lautens, Trevor. "Ottawa Angling to Dump Monarchy." *North Shore News* 29 Nov. 1999: 1.

Leavis, F.R. *Mass Civilization and Minority Culture.* Cambridge: Minority, 1930.

Lewis, Robert. "Who Says the GG Has to Be Boring." *Maclean's* 20 Sept. 1999: 2.

Lewis, Robert, and Bruce Wallace. "The View from Rideau Hall." *Maclean's* 27 Dec. 1999: 210.

Ling, Amy. *Yellow Light: The Flowering of Asian American Arts.* Philadelphia: Temple UP, 1999.

Lorinc, John. "Diatribe Dip." Rev. of *The Doubter's Companion*, by John Ralston Saul. *Quill and Quire* Oct. 1994: 31.

Lownsbrough, John. "Uncommon Sense: John Ralston Saul Aims to Turn Our Turbulent Times into Another Age of Enlightenment." *Books in Canada* Dec. 1993: 8–14.

Maddox, Susan, and Paula Weber. "Famous Mothers and Babies—Can You Tell Who's Whose?" *Chatelaine* July 1972, 35, 44.

"The Man Behind the Book." Rev. of *On Equilibrium*, by John Ralston Saul. *Ottawa Citizen* 16 Dec. 2001: C13.

Marchand, Philip. "Why the Literati Aren't Gaga over the GG." *Toronto Star* 18 Sept. 1999: J4.

Martin, Lawrence. "But Watch for Big Changes." *Calgary Herald* 11 Sept. 1999: O55.

——. "A Fine Week to Wave Our Flag." *Victoria Times-Colonist* 1 Feb. 2001: A10.

——. "The Price We Pay for Quality." *Vancouver Sun* 19 Oct. 1999: A19.

Martin, Sandra. "Adrienne Clarkson on Switching Careers." *Canadian Living* 29 Oct. 1988: 62.

McCracken, Melinda. "The Dream of Adrienne Clarkson." *Maclean's* Sept. 1972: 32–33, 60–66.

REFERENCES

McGinnis, Rick. "The Diary Thing." 4 May 2002. <rickmcginnis.com>

McGoogan, Kenneth. "Author Completes Wrap of Southeast Asia Set." *Calgary Herald* 14 June 1988: E67.

McGregor, Glen. "Clarkson Spent $27,000 on Flights, Limos and Lunch." *National Post* 18 Oct. 1999: A1, A2.

McIlroy, Anne. "Canada Greets Clarkson at Last." *Globe and Mail* 8 Oct. 1999: A1, A3.

McLennan, Ross. "The Lady Oughta Zip Her Lip." *Winnipeg Sun* 20 Oct. 1999: 11.

Melnyk, George. "Saul Lambastes Voltaire's Bastards." *Calgary Herald* 26 Sept. 1992: D12.

Moher, Frank. "The Writer She Didn't Quote: Clarkson's Own Fiction." *National Post* 9 Oct. 1999: B1, B10.

Moore, Christopher. "John Ralston Saul: Reforming Canada's History." Rev. of *Reflections of a Siamese Twin*, by John Ralston Saul. *The Beaver* 78:3 (1998): 51–52.

Moore, Lynn, and Sid Adilman. "Women in Power Urged to Give More Jobs to Women." *Toronto Star* 8 Nov. 1986: A15.

Morrow, Martin. "On the Go: CBC's Ambassador of the Arts Adrienne Clarkson Keeps Canadians in the Know." *Calgary Herald* 28 June 1992: D1.

Mulawka, Brian. "Who Will Curtsey, The Queen or Adrienne? Governor General Clarkson Does Lack the Imperious Impulse." *British Columbia Report* 23 Sept. 1999: 32.

Naumetz, Tim. "Reform Takes Another Shot at 'Madame Clarkson.'" *Calgary Herald* 6 Nov. 1999: A2.

Newman, Peter C. "Inventing Canada." Rev. of *Reflections of a Siamese Twin*, by John Ralston Saul. *Maclean's* 15 Dec. 1997: 68.

Oleson, Tom. "A Rude Awakening in Thailand." Rev. of *The Paradise Eater*, by John Ralston Saul. *Winnipeg Free Press* 18 June 1988: 56.

"105 Potential Women MPs." *Chatelaine* Oct. 1971: 33–38.

O'Neill. Juliet. "Broadcaster Named as Governor General." *Calgary Herald* 9 Sept. 1999: A3.

——. "Clarkson Defends Husband's Title, Anti-U.S. Remarks." *Calgary Herald* 29 Jan. 2002: A4.

——. "Clarkson's Entry to Canada." *Vancouver Sun* 10 Sept. 1999: A15.

Peate, Les. "Many Questions—Few Answers." *Esprit de Corps* Mar. 1998: 11–12.

Penny, Laura. "Figure Head to Head. *Toronto Life* June 2000: 12.

Persky, Stan. "What's Wrong with Reason, Anyway?" Rev. of *Voltaire's Bastards*, by John Ralston Saul. *Globe and Mail* 12 Sept. 1992: C22.

"Publishers Appoint Clarkson." *Chronicle-Herald* [Halifax] 8 Nov. 1986: 47.

Reiss, Timothy. *The Discourse of Modernism.* Ithaca: Cornell UP, 1982.

Robertson, Heather. "Television." *Maclean's* Jan. 1973: 68.

Roper, Gordon. Rev. of *A Lover More Condoling*, by Adrienne Clarkson. *University of Toronto Quarterly* 38 (1969): 359.

Ross, Val. "A Visionary in Our Midst." *Globe and Mail* 25 Feb. 1995: C21.

Ryan, Leo. "Canadian Author Shakes up France with Death Tale." *Globe and Mail* 15 July 1977: 7.

Sagar, Dorianne. "Sticks and Stones: Is the Media Getting Meaner?" *Thunderbird: UBC Journalism Review* Nov. 1999. <www.journalism. ubc.ca/thunderbird/2000/october>

Saul, John Ralston. Archived speeches.

——. *Baraka.* Toronto: Granada, 1983.

——. *The Birds of Prey.* London: Macmillan, 1977.

——. *The Doubter's Companion: A Dictionary of Aggressive Common Sense.* Toronto: Penguin, 1994.

——. *The Next Best Thing.* Toronto: Collins, 1986.

——. *On Equilibrium.* Toronto: Penguin, 2001.

——. *The Paradise Eater.* Toronto: Random House, 1988.

——. *Reflections of a Siamese Twin: Canada at the End of the Twentieth Century.* Toronto: Viking, 1997.

——. *The Unconscious Civilization.* Toronto: Anansi, 1995.

——. *Voltaire's Bastards: The Dictatorship of Reason in the West.* New York: Free Press, 1992.

"Saul Respects Limits of His Role." Editorial. *Edmonton Journal* 21 Dec. 2001: A18.

"Saul's Timing Bad, But His Argument Is Even Worse." Editorial. *Calgary Sun* 21 Dec. 2001: A6.

"Saul's View: A Misdirected Controversy." Editorial. *Sudbury Star* 19 Dec. 2001: A10.

Schnurmacher, Thomas. "Thriller Cast Postures in the Jungles of Asia." Rev. of *The Next Best Thing*, by John Ralston Saul. *Gazette* [Montreal] 26 July 1986: B8.

Sexton, Rosemary. "Adrienne Clarkson's Painful Separation." *National Post* 6 Nov. 1999: B7.

——. "A Sense of Panache at Rideau Hall." *National Post* 11 Sept. 1999: B7.

Shannon, Norman. "The Contempt of Senate." *Esprit de Corps* Mar. 1998: 12.

"Shopaholic GG Binges Again." *Frank* 3 Oct. 2001: 3.

Sidebar. *National Post* 8 Oct. 1999: A3.

Simpson, Jeffrey. "The Two-Headed Governor-General." *Globe and Mail* 9 Sept. 1999: A14.

Steed, Judy. "An Immigrant's Rise to Be Governor-General." *Toronto Star* 6 Oct. 1999: A1, A6.

Steyn, Mark. "Long Live Queen Adrienne." *National Post* 16 Sept. 1999: A18.

——. "The Prince Consort Has No Clothes." *National Post* 20 Dec. 2001: A20.

Swift, Jamie. "The Last Intellectual." Rev. of *Reflections of a Siamese Twin*, by John Ralston Saul. *Queen's Quarterly* 105:1 (1998): 65–71.

"Thank You, Madame Clarkson." Editorial. *Globe and Mail* 11 Oct. 1999: A8.

Valpy, Michael. "Expect High Profile and a Sense of Style." *Globe and Mail* 9 Sept. 1999: A2.

Ward, Olivia. "It's So Nice to Be John Ralston Saul." *Toronto Star* 18 Mar. 1979: D1, D7.

Ward, Sheila. "The French Connection." *Metropolitan Toronto Business Journal* Jan.-Feb. 1984: 22–26.

Warren, David. "Intellectual Fraud Parades as Genius." *Ottawa Citizen* 28 Oct. 1999: A19.

——. "That's Saul Folks." Rev. of *The Unconscious Civilization*, by John Ralston Saul. *Saturday Night* June 1996: 23–24.

Watkins, Mel. "With Clarkson at Her Swearing-In." *Now* 14–20 Oct. 1999: 3.

Waugh, Neil. "That's Saul, Folks." Editorial. *Edmonton Sun,* 22 Dec. 2001: 10.

Webster, Norman. "Stars Shine at Rideau Hall." Editorial. *Gazette* [Montreal] 11 Sept. 1999: B7.

Wigod, Rebecca. "Having Pointed Out Civilization's Discontents, John Ralston Saul Hints at Solutions." *Vancouver Sun* 15 Dec. 2001: H15.

Wigston, Nancy. "East and West." *Books in Canada* June-July 1988: 19–21.

Williams, Raymond. *Marxism and Literature.* Oxford: Oxford UP, 1977.

Winsor, Hugh. "A Predictable Choice and an Easy Name for Journalists to Spell." *Globe and Mail* 8 Sept. 1999: A3.

Wiseman, Nelson. Rev. of *Reflections of a Siamese Twin*, by John Ralston Saul. *Quill and Quire* Nov. 1997: 30.

Wong, Jan. "On Madame Clarkson Playing the Chinese Card." *Globe and Mail* 8 Oct. 1999: A24.

——. "Says 'She's Adrienne Clarkson, And I'm Not.'" *Globe and Mail* 10 Sept. 1999: A20.

Woodcock, Connie. "The G.G.: Who Really Cares?" *Toronto Sun* 11 Sept. 1999: 15.

Woodcock, George. "Ravaged by the Technocrats." Rev. of *Voltaire's Bastards*, by John Ralston Saul. *Quill and Quire* Aug. 1992: 20.

Yaffe, Barbara. "Forget the Pomp: Clarkson Should Recognize Our Circumstance." *Vancouver Sun* 21 Oct. 1999: A23.

Yanofsky, Joel. "Bangkok Blues." Rev. of *The Paradise Eater*, by John Ralston Saul. *Gazette* [Montreal] 11 June 1988: L12.

——. "The Novel According to John Ralston Saul." *Gazette* [Montreal] 11 June 1988: L12.

Zerbesias, Antonia. "Adrienne Clarkson on Art, Life, and Invisibility." *Toronto Star* 17 June 1989: H3.

Index

INDEX

INDEX